THE GREAT
MAHJONG
BOOK

THE GREAT
MAHJONG
BOOK

HISTORY, LORE, AND PLAY
Jelte Rep

TUTTLE Publishing

Tokyo | Rutland, Vermont | Singapore

"Books to Span the East and West"

Tuttle Publishing was founded in 1832 in the small New England town of Rutland, Vermont [USA]. Our core values remain as strong today as they were then—to publish best-in-class books which bring people together one page at a time. In 1948, we established a publishing office in Japan—and Tuttle is now a leader in publishing English-language books about the arts, languages and cultures of Asia. The world has become a much smaller place today and Asia's economic and cultural influence has grown. Yet the need for meaningful dialogue and information about this diverse region has never been greater. Over the past seven decades, Tuttle has published thousands of books on subjects ranging from martial arts and paper crafts to language learning and literature—and our talented authors, illustrators, designers and photographers have won many prestigious awards. We welcome you to explore the wealth of information available on Asia at **www.tuttlepublishing.com**.

Published by Tuttle Publishing,
an imprint of Periplus Editions (HK) Ltd.

www.tuttlepublishing.com

Copyright © 2007 Jelte Rep

A translation into English of *Het Groot Mahjong Boek: Alle spelsoorten, achtergronden en geschiedenis* by Jelte Rep, originally published in Dutch by Tirion Uitgevers B.V. in 2003.

Library of Congress Cataloging-in-Publication Data

Rep, Jelte, 1940–
  [Groot Mahjong Boek. English]
  The great mahjong book : history, lore and play / Jelte Rep. — 1st ed.
    224p. : ill. (some col.) : 23 cm.
  Includes index.
  ISBN 0-8048-3719-8 (pbk.)
  1. Mah jong—History. I. Title.
  GV1299.M3R4613 2007
  795.3'4—dc22   2006022245

ISBN 978-0-8048-3719-4

Distributed by

North America, Latin America and Europe
Tuttle Publishing
364 Innovation Drive, North Clarendon,
VT 05759-9436 U.S.A.
Tel: (802) 773 8930
Fax: (802) 773 6993
info@tuttlepublishing.com
www.tuttlepublishing.com

Asia Pacific
Berkeley Books Pte Ltd
3 Kallang Sector #04-01,
Singapore 349278
Tel: (65) 6741-2178
Fax: (65) 67414-2179
inquiries@periplus.com.sg
www.tuttlepublishing.com

Japan
Tuttle Publishing
Yaekari Building, 3rd Floor
5-4-12 Osaki, Shinagawa-ku
Tokyo 141 0032
Tel: (81) 3 5437-0171
Fax: (81) 3 5437-0755
sales@tuttle.co.jp
www.tuttle.co.jp

25 24 23 22 21   10 9 8 7 6 5   2106VP   Printed in Malaysia

TUTTLE PUBLISHING® is a registered trademark of Tuttle Publishing, a division of Periplus Editions (HK) Ltd.

CONTENTS

A wooden mahjong case

THE FIRST TIME

It was a long time ago now, but I can still remember in great detail the night when a friend placed a mysterious small box on the table in front of me and opened the lid with an excited gesture. It was a cold winter evening. Outside an east wind sucked all the warmth out of a body, but inside a bottle of wine and a fired-up stove warmed us.

The box contained rectangular tiles with mysterious symbols and equally incomprehensible Chinese characters. My friend turned the box over and the tiles clattered toward me. There must have been over one hundred, maybe even two hundred. I leaned closer to look at the mysterious tiles. The unmistakable smell of the Far East came up. If they were laid facedown, the tiles looked like small white breads with a well baked, dark brown encrustation, but if they were turned faceup, they showed small miniatures, refined and engraved in ivory . . .

("Synthetic material," my friend corrected later.)

. . . and soberly colored with red, green, and blue. On certain tiles an unknown master hand had cut beautiful flowers, and on other tiles there was no illustration at all.

"What is this?" I asked excitedly.

"Mahjong," he replied with a grin.

That very wintry night I became addicted to the game. It became more and more miraculous and thrilling. There were Winds and Dragons, Circles, Characters, and Bamboos. Those nice flowers proved to be seasons but were pushed aside with contempt. Later he would explain to me why they were treated so. First we had to build a square and immediately thereafter tear it down by rolling the smallest dice I had ever seen. These Lilliputians decided our destiny, because the place where the wall was broken was decisive for the course of the game, my friend explained. Uneasily I picked up my first thirteen tiles and began to play with uncertainty. It dazzled me. How could I ever absorb all those rules and distinguish all those tiles?

"What is this, for heaven's sake?"

"Pe-ling!"

"Pe-what?"

"That is bird Pe-ling. Or 1-Bamboo-1 for dummies."

"And what is this? It has nothing on it?"

"That is the White Dragon."

The evening became night. The uncertainty became passion. I discovered that mahjong is not a difficult game at all, that you can force luck from time to time, and that the tiles bring surprise after surprise. I entered an exotic world with odd symbols, painstaking rituals, and centuries-old traditions in which Dragons emerge at most unexpected moments and the Winds reverse course. When late that night my friend said goodbye to me in the ice-cold east wind, I knew that there is no more beautiful, no more thrilling, and no more exciting game than mahjong.

"What does it actually mean?" I asked, chattering.

"Mahjong? The game of a hundred wonders."

And though my friend taught me some incorrect plays, which I later had to unlearn, I remain grateful to him for inaugurating me on that icy wintry night in the temptations and the rituals of the game of mahjong, indeed a game of one hundred wonders.

INTRODUCTION:
GAME OF ONE HUNDRED WONDERS

In Chinese, it is pronounced *Ma-chur,* in which the *r* is a guttural sound that also sounds very much like an unstressed *e.* There are many more spelling variations: Mah-dsjangg, Mah-dshiongg, Mo-dsjiang, Ma-dsjongg, Ma-tsiang, Ma-chian, Majiang, Ma-jack, Ma-yong, Ma-jong, Ma-tsuie, Ma-tsiang, Ma-tsiong, Ma-chiao, Ma-tsuerh, Mah-jongg, Majiang. This book sticks simply to mahjong.

Mahjong can be played in hundreds of ways. In China it is played differently than in America, in Japan differently than in Hong Kong, in Great Britain differently than in France, in one region differently than in another, and in the Johnsons' house differently than the Steiners' house.

You can compare it with playing cards, which can be played in hundreds of ways. It is the same with mahjong—with the same tiles you can play in countless different ways. It doesn't matter what version you play since mahjong remains a special and exciting game no matter how it is played.

This book describes the many ways in which mahjong can be played and how many interesting additions or simplifications are possible. It is written for the beginning and for the experienced mahjong player and is a guide as well as a reference book. You are encouraged to play mahjong in the way that appeals to you most and with the rules that excite you most; you will also find the rules you need to obey if you want to become the champion of the world.

The starting point of this book is mahjong the way it was played by the Chinese more than a century ago, before it was discovered by the West. After that, the rules and variants are presented that were added everywhere in the world, where the game created a furor. *The Great Mahjong Book* shows why mahjong is often called the game of one hundred wonders and the game of ten thousand possibilities.

Tiles

To begin to understand mahjong, you must become familiar with its many components. A complete mahjong set usually contains 144 tiles, but often four and sometimes eight tiles more, in addition to some accessories. First let's look at the different types of tiles. They can be divided as follows:

Circles

Numbered from 1 through 9, four tiles of each number, for a total of thirty-six.

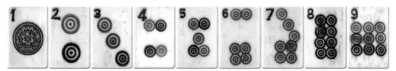

Circle-1 through Circle-9

The Circles are also called "dots" or "balls." Since counting sticks contain "dots," I prefer to refer to these tiles as Circles.

Bamboos

Numbered from 1 through 9, four tiles of each number, for a total of thirty-six.

1-Bamboo through 9-Bamboo

1-Bamboo is remarkable; on it a mythical bird called Pe-ling is depicted, which in Chinese means "beautiful singing." However, the bird depicted is not always a Chinese songbird, but most often a peacock, pheasant, or a sparrow.

Characters

Numbered from 1 through 9, four tiles of each number, for a total of thirty-six.

1-Character through 9-Character

The lower red ideograph represents the number ten thousand. The upper part consists of the numbers 1 through 9, so the Character tiles represent the numbers ten thousand through ninety thousand in Chinese.

Dragons
Dragons consist of Red Dragons (often indicated with the letter *C*), Green Dragons (indicated by *F*), and White Dragons (indicated by *P* or *B*). There are four of each tile, for a total of twelve.

The Red, Green, and White Dragons

The Chinese Characters on the Dragon tiles are Chung (middle) for the Red Dragon, Fa (growth) for the Green Dragon, and Po (blank) for the White Dragon. In some sets, completely blank tiles serve as White Dragons.

Winds
Winds consist of the East Wind (often indicated with the letter *E*), the South Wind (indicated by the letter *S*), the West Wind (indicated by the letter *W*), and the North Wind (indicated by the letter *N*). There are four of each tile, for a total of sixteen.

The Four Winds

Bonus Tiles
There are eight bonus tiles, which are subdivided in two groups of four tiles, and are differentiated by the color of their numbers—one group has red numbers, the other green. The numbers of the tiles correspond with the seats of the four players. The number 1 belongs to East, 2 to South, 3 to West, and 4 to North. The tiles are not used to build hands (they do not form Pungs or Chows), but are used as counters for special bonuses (or penalties) applied to players.

The two groups of bonus tiles

The Chinese artisans have indulged their fantasies on the bonus tiles. The result is that the bonus tiles are not uniform in style or content. The only distinction between the two sets is the color of the Chinese characters.

The pictures vary from set to set and are not easily distinguished from each other. Sometimes flowers and seasons are depicted, sometimes flowers are used exclusively, and at other times there are no flowers at all. The following are some themes: wind-flower-snow-moon; fisher-woodcutter-farmer-master; music playing–chess playing–writing–painting; and Chinese means of transport (handcart-sedan-rickshaw-junk) or structures (bridge-gate-pavilion-pagoda).

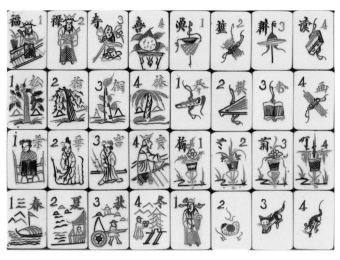

The Chinese tile carver can indulge his craft on the bonus tiles, creating the most beautiful decorations. This set from 1925, destined for export to America, has thirty-two different bonus tiles.

For Westerners, the characters on the bonus tiles are cryptic. The characters in each series often form a strophe from a poem that the engraver liked or that he felt he could easily appropriate. The two strophes have nothing to do with the bonus tiles they decorate. Because the bonus tiles give the engraver the opportunity to indulge his craftsmanship, fantasy, and artistic feelings, they are the most beautiful of the whole set.

The bonus tiles are also called The Eight Apostles by the Chinese, a reference to the eight immortal followers of the great Chinese philosopher Lao Tse (from the second century B.C.E.) who, through their ascetic and devout practice, became saints in their kingdom of heaven.

The modern Western versions are much more prosaic. They have clear texts and numbers and much less beautiful pictures. They represent the four seasons—spring, summer, autumn, and winter—and four matching flowers—plum, orchid, chrysanthemum, and bamboo.

Bonus tiles in Western presentation. They are often called "flowers" and "seasons."

Numbering the tiles is not always done in the same way. Sometimes the bamboo flower carries number 3 and the chrysanthemum number 4, while in other sets the bamboo flower is number 2 and the orchid is number 4. The season tiles carry blue characters and the flower tiles red ones, but this rule is sometimes broken. This does not affect the game as long as the bonus tiles form two clear groups and are easy recognizable by the players.

	Season	Flower	Belongs to
1	Spring	Plum	East
2	Summer	Orchid	South
3	Autumn	Chrysanthemum	West
4	Winter	Bamboo	North

Spare Tiles

Better mahjong sets have four blank tiles on which the picture of a lost tile can be engraved. If an engraver is too expensive or not available, a pair of good felt-tip pens can work. Sometimes the blank tiles are identical to the White Dragons. In that case, it is wise to use the blank tiles and the White Dragons alternately so that they lose color at the same pace as the other tiles; this will keep them from becoming too easily recognizable in case they should replace a lost tile later.

In addition to tiles, a mahjong set contains the following accessories:

Dice

Mahjong requires just two dice (most sets include four). They are unusually small and differ from standard dice by their differing faces. The 1 is represented by a red or blank hole and the four dots of the 4 are colored red instead of black.

Dice with a red four and a red one

Why the Dice Have Red Eyes

The Chinese consider red an auspicious color and therefore they like to decorate their daily durable articles with a small strike of red paint. What is considered the best throw of a die, the one, is thus auspiciously colored red.

The origin of the red four has a colorful story. Emperor Hsuan Tsung from the Chinese Tang-dynasty played dice with Yang Kuei-Feit, his concubine, and had to throw three consecutive fours to win. The first throw was good, the second also. The court watched in tension. Four, four, begged the emperor, before he dared to throw the die for the third time. The die fulfilled the fiery wish of the emperor. A courtier, who had watched in tension with the others, proposed to mark this special event, on which the emperor decreed that in the future the four on every die should be colored red, the color of luck.

Counting Sticks

Players use counting sticks to settle their scores. These counters have different values. There is a great variety of counting sticks, depending on where the mahjong set comes from.

The Chinese counting sticks are often made of bone and are recognizable by their irregular form. They are also called counters, tallies, or bones. Chinese sets should have at least 116 sticks.

The Eyes of the Sticks

The eyes of the Chinese elongated counting sticks are there for a reason: they have
a symbolic value. They represent heaven,
earth, humanity, and harmony.

Chinese counting sticks

Number	Value	Dots
8	500	6 red and 6 black
36	100	2 red
32	10	8 red
40	2	1 red and 3 black

The counting stick of 500 points counts
six red and six black eyes, twelve in total—the number of perfection. The six red
and the six black eyes represent the balance within that perfection. You cannot
achieve a higher goal.

The counting stick of 100 points counts
two red eyes and points to a high grade of perfection. Two is, after all, the number of completeness, the perfect couple.

The eight eyes on **the counting stick of 10
points** symbolize the eight many-sided apostles of the great Lao Tse, who together reached a high degree of perfection. Therefore eight is a holy number in China.

The counting stick of 2 points with the
one red eye and the three slanted black eyes points to the seemingly contradicto-
ry nature of the animal kingdom with its harmony, despite its imbalance. The
one animal overpowers the other, but still all the species continue to exist. In
Chinese astrology, harmony unites heaven, earth, and humanity.

The number of eyes and their names are taken from the Chinese domino game in which the highest throws are double-six, double-one, double-four, and three-by-one.

The mahjong sets that are imported from China to the West usually contain counting sticks of synthetic material. They represent higher values, because in the West, mahjong is played for more points than in its country of origin. There are 84 counting sticks in total.

Amount	Value	Dots
4	1000	5 red and 2 black
8	500	5 red
32	100	1 red
40	10	8 black

If your mahjong set does not contain counting sticks, then you can resort to the plastic chips that are used in poker or roulette games. To the chips of which you have the most, you assign the lowest value, usually 2 points, but sometimes 100 points. To the chips of which you have the least, you assign the highest value: 500 or 4000 points.

To link the colors on your plastic chips to Chinese symbols, and to help you remember which value they represent, I suggest using this color scheme:

Amount	Color	Represents	Value	Or
8	yellow	gold	500	4000
36	blue	heaven	100	1000
32	red	luck	10	500
40	white	prosperity	2	100

It doesn't matter what your counting chips look like or what value you give them. Their purpose is to help you easily settle your points with the other players. If your sticks are exhausted during the game, you can buy sticks from one of the winning players using a written IOU.

Mahjong Racks

Mahjong racks are another very handy accessory. They help with the building of the wall and angle your tiles for easy viewing during the game. One of the racks has a different color and is reserved for the player with the East Wind. Mahjong racks come in many varieties. They're rarely sold with a mahjong set and are usually purchased separately. When buying a rack, try your tiles on it first to make sure they don't stand too upright, which will make them difficult to see. And take good care that the racks are not bent, since this will make them spin around, which can be a great source of annoyance (a counting stick slid under one of the bent ends offers a temporary solution).

East distinguishes itself from the other players with the red mahjong rack.

Racks that are seventeen or eighteen tiles long are most convenient—depending on the variant you like to play—because their length facilitates the building of the wall, which is something you have to do very often during a game.

The Chinese don't use mahjong racks. Instead, they place their tiles upright in front of them, just like domino tiles. But Chinese tiles are considerably larger than the mahjong tiles that are used in most parts of the West, making them much more stable. They will not fall easily when they are placed upright.

Ming Box

The ming box is a small tube, containing four little discs on which the four winds are indicated (in Chinese characters). They are not necessary to the game. Players can use these discs to indicate which Wind they will be in the game. The empty ming box is placed near the player who started the game as East. The Wind discs can also be used to decide the seating arrangement of the players around the table.

A ming box with four Wind discs

A modern variant of the ming box is the plastic ming disc; it contains a die on which the four Winds, the Green Dragon, and the Red Dragon are stamped. The die indicates the prevailing Wind and is always placed next to the player who is East.

Modern ming discs

Other handy variants have a revolving disc or cone, with which you can indicate the prevailing Wind.

Most desirable of all, however, is a ming or Wind disc on which all the Wind directions are marked, making it a constant indicator of your present Wind. A piece of paper with the four Wind directions written on it will do as well. A Wind disc is easy to make yourself. My father, who never saw anything in that odd game of mahjong, generously fabricated a nice Wind disc out of wood on my instructions. To this day, that Wind disc accompanies every game I play at home. The four Chinese Wind directions are marked on its foot. By turning the disc you indicate that the prevailing Wind has changed.

The Wind disc my father fabricated for me out of wood

Buying a Mahjong Set

Every sort of mahjong set is available for sale and in a range of prices. They vary from expensive ivory specimens of colored tiles with delicate hand engraving that are arranged in drawers in beautiful rosewood or lacquer boxes, to molded and stamped plastic pieces in thrifty colors and packed in shabby synthetic cases. There is a set for every purse.

Sets of gemstone, like this one of white jade, are rarities. The Chinese consider jade a valuable gift from heaven and their craftsmen are very skillful in working with this precious stone.

If possible, don't be too economical when purchasing a mahjong set. A nice mahjong set heightens the pleasure of playing. A good mahjong set has to possess tiles that are easy to pick up, feel fine in your hand, and are easy to distinguish. Check that a set is complete and contains at least 144 tiles, two dice, and a set of counting chips or sticks. Examine the back of the tiles to make sure that they all look the same. One recognizable tile makes the whole set worthless.

Ivory or Bone

Mahjong sets are made of all kinds of materials. The new sets are generally produced of synthetic material and the pictures are stamped and therefore coarse. There are also bamboo sets for sale. They weigh little and are often somewhat round in shape, which makes them hard to stack up. Their pictures are usually not so delicate because bamboo is difficult to engrave.

In the 1930s, Bakelite was used as a material for mahjong tiles. These tiles range in color from creamy white to pitch-black but were dark yellow most of the time. The pictures are stamped but sometimes also engraved by hand.

Most vintage sets are made of bone with bamboo on the back. Sometimes ebony is used instead of bamboo. Purveyors of mahjong sets will sometimes try to sell bone sets as ivory. To discern bone from ivory a strong loupe and a good light source are needed to study the structure thoroughly. Ivory doesn't have filaments but has fine rhomboidal veins and a layered structure. It is much harder than bone. Since 1990, there has been a worldwide ban on trade in raw ivory to protect its producer, the African elephant, against extinction. Ivory from the already extinct Mammoth elephant can still be traded, but it is of lesser quality.

Mahjong tiles of ivory are rare and expensive. Moreover, these pieces have a back of ebony, which makes them entirely exceptional. Bone tiles are often presented and sold as ivory.

How Mahjong Sets Were Made

Before the West showed its insatiable interest in mahjong, the Chinese made sets in small workshops using methods that passed from father to son and were refined from generation to generation. Every workshop had its own specialty. One workshop cut and sawed the bone used for the front of the tiles into flat pieces. Another workshop dried the bamboo and sawed it into small blocks. A third one put the bone fronts and bamboo backs together to form the tiles, and the fourth one did the engraving. This work was done by fathers, grandfathers, and great-grandfathers, and so it would perhaps still be done if the Great Mahjong Craze had not broken out. It seemed that everyone in

Tiles from a vintage mahjong set. Bone and bamboo are tightly joined with a handmade dovetail fitting.

the West wanted to own a mahjong set and American businessmen burned to fulfill that demand. But the Chinese shrugged their shoulders and refused to work harder than their fathers, grandfathers, and great-grandfathers did just because crazy foreigners suddenly wanted to play their game. Moreover, they said, there was simply not enough bone to produce so many tiles.

Mahjong tiles are made from the shinbone of a cow, and one mahjong set requires sixteen shin bones. Impossible, the Chinese said. Nothing is impossible, the Americans said, and they exported shiploads of cow legs from the slaughterhouses of Chicago to China.

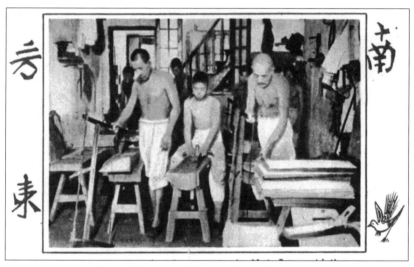

Here workers are sawing wood for mahjong boxes.

Recruiting workers to make mahjong tiles out of those legs was a considerably more difficult problem to solve. The Chinese appeared not willing to leave their workshops and villages to work in a factory. In despair, enterprising British and Americans bought complete workshops and moved them to Shanghai. The workers were appeased with high premiums and bonuses, a guaranteed minimum wage, and room and board. In this way the Mei Ren Company became prominent in Shanghai, in which fifteen old-fashioned workshops from places like Soochow, Wenchow, Hangchow, Yangchow and Ningbo were dismantled and reassembled together. Henceforth the whole working line, from constructing the mahjong boxes through the packaging of the mahjong sets, happened quickly and efficiently under one roof. Only the bamboo, which had to be dried for at least eighteen months, was delivered by Chinese dealers pre-sawed into rectangular pieces of the desired size.

The handicraft remained as it had always been. The bone was bleached until it was snow white and after that one of the craftsmen cut it with a primitive saw into small pieces measuring about 1½ inches in length (4 cm). A number of men beside him cleaved the pieces into two or three parts with a lump of wood and an iron chisel.

Another group of artisans cut the pieces of bone by hand into flat parts. Next the thickness was measured. The thicker the bone, the more expensive the mahjong set. On average, one or two thick tiles came from one piece of shinbone.

After that the bone front and the bamboo back were joined with dovetail fitting. This precise job was done only with a file and a hammer and it happened so fast that you hardly could follow it. In the bone a groove was made for the tail, which projected from the bamboo. The two parts fit so precisely together that you could hardly see the joint.

Then the tile was filed by hand and the corners beveled. After that the tiles were clamped together in a line to be polished—first with a piece of sandpaper, then with a hard piece of fish skin, and finally with reed or other plants—until their faces were

Chinese workers polishing mahjong tiles

as smooth and even as glass and felt pleasing to the touch. Then the thickness of the tiles was measured and the tiles were sorted by their thickness to form a complete set: 150 tiles in total (including spare tiles).

After that the tiles were engraved. The Circles were applied with a primitive hand drill. The Bamboos and the Characters were engraved by hand by boys aged from twelve to eighteen years, each of whom had his own specialty—Bamboos, Characters, Circles, Winds, or Dragons.

The tiles were painted with locally-available colors: red, dark purple, and brown. The paint was applied liberally to the tile and then wiped off with a cloth, so that the paint remained only in the engraved parts. Errant paint drops were removed from the engravings with a small, sharp chisel. Now the tiles were finished and were put into the small drawers of the wooden mahjong boxes, which were made in the same factory. Quick hands wrapped up the boxes and the mahjong sets were hurried to the harbor of Shanghai for export to America and Great Britain.

THE BASIC RULES OF MAHJONG

Just like a set of cards, a set of mahjong tiles can be played in many ways. All the playing variants have their own rules, peculiarities, and appeal. Besides that, many house or club rules circulate. If you're invited for a game of mahjong, then it is necessary to inquire which variant will be played. Yet, despite their differences, all these variations on the game are based on the same basic rules. If you are just learning to play mahjong, you should start with these.

Winds

To play mahjong, you need four players, or "Winds" as they are referred to in mahjong-speak. The players bear the names of the four Wind directions: East, South, West, and North. For that reason mahjong is also called the Game of the Four Winds. Just as in nature, the four Winds have fixed places in relation to each other. However, in mahjong, South is to the right of East, not to the left.

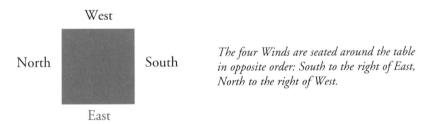

The four Winds are seated around the table in opposite order: South to the right of East, North to the right of West.

Playing Direction

This order proves once more that mahjong is a heavenly game. If you think about where South and East are located, you'll notice that East is to the right of South, and that you have to move counterclockwise to go from East to South. Mahjong is played against the direction of the clock, from East to South to West to North.

Four Rounds, or Winds

A complete game of mahjong consists of four rounds, also called Winds. Each Wind consists of at least four games, which are also often called hands. So a minimum of sixteen hands is played. It is not necessary to finish a whole game in one session. You can agree on a time limit or on a certain number of hands and pick up where you left off the next time you play. Make sure the agreement to continue the game later is clear to all since the players who are losing generally prefer to start a new game.

Prevailing Wind

During each round there is a prevailing Wind. In the first round East is the prevailing Wind, in the second round the South Wind prevails, in the third round the West Wind, and in the fourth round the North Wind.

The East Wind is the most important Wind of the play, because East starts each game and each round. The East player scores double for a completed hand and pays double when paying sticks for an opponent's completed hand. Variants on this rule are possible.

In view of his special position East is often called the Banker, the Dealer, or the Eldest. The title East passes from player to player. As soon as the first player (the player who was East first) becomes East again, the next round begins, and the prevailing Wind changes. When the East round ends, the South round begins.

Sticks

The counting sticks are distributed. The variant you play determines how many sticks you will get and which value they represent.

Seating Arrangements

Before playing can begin, the seating is randomized to ensure fairness. Which player begins as East is also randomized. This way, all players have an equal chance. A randomly chosen seat can have a harmful influence on your game. It can give evil spirits a chance to ruin your hand and chase away your good luck.

The opening ceremony differs from playing variant to playing variant. The older the playing variant, the more elaborate the ritual. In the modern playing variants, the ceremony is reduced to picking up one of the four Wind tiles, which are laid facedown on the table.

By choosing from the four facedown Wind tiles, you determine the Wind with which you will start the game and who you will sit next to at the table.

Tip: It is wise to carry out the opening ceremony with careful attentiveness. This is done out of respect for the game and for mahjong ghosts, who never skip a game.

Building the Wall

When you play with the bonus tiles the game counts 144 tiles—without them there are 136 tiles in the game. The inclusion of bonus tiles depends on the playing variant and/or the preferences of the players.

At the beginning of each game, the tiles are placed face down and shuffled thoroughly. Shuffling is done carefully, since the tiles can be chipped. However, the shuffling can make quite a racket, especially when it is done on a bare table. The Chinese therefore call this ceremony the twittering of the sparrows.

After placing the tiles facedown on the table, the tiles are thoroughly shuffled by two opposite players or by all four players.

After the tiles are shuffled, each player builds a wall of facedown tiles with a length of eighteen tiles (if you play with the bonus tiles) or seventeen tiles (without the bonus tiles) and a height of two tiles. The four walls are pushed toward each other to form a square. The right side of each wall, however, should jut out from the square. This goes easier with mahjong racks, which are typically used in the West. When you play with large tiles, which easily stand upright, racks are unnecessary. The square symbolizes the Great Wall of China.

Tip: To give evil spirits no chance to interfere with what will happen among the four walls, it is advisable to build a sealed square.

Distinguishing East

East has to show clearly that he is the leader of the game. This can be accomplished in a number of different ways. He can place the ming box clearly in front of him. The Wind of each player is indicated on frequently-used Wind discs.

Additionally, since the rack of the East is a different color (mostly red) from the other Winds, this too can be used to distinguish East from other Winds.

The closed wall with four sides of seventeen tiles each. The bonus tiles are not used in this game.

Breaking the Wall

Which wall will be broken, and where, is determined randomly. There are several methods for determining this, depending on the variant you play.

In most variants, East throws two dice and the number rolled decides whose wall will be broken. East counts counterclockwise the number of the dice roll, beginning with himself:

Number Rolled			Wall Broken
2	6	10	South
3	7	11	West
4	8	12	North
5	9		East

If, for example, East throws a 7, West's wall will be broken.

After that, the player whose wall will be broken rolls the dice. He takes the number he rolls and adds it to the number East rolled. So, for example, if West throws 6, he adds it to the 7 East rolled, for a total of 13. West then counts thirteen tiles, starting from his right, and breaks the wall between the thirteenth and fourteenth tiles.

The two tiles that are chosen randomly to be removed from the wall are placed to the right of the opening in this order: the bottom tile closest to the break, followed by the upper tile. These two tiles are called loose tiles, and they lay on the dead wall. The tiles in the dead wall, usually consisting of fourteen tiles, are not used in the game (except to deal players replacement tiles). Variants on this rule are possible.

The broken wall with the two loose tiles on the dead wall

Dealing the Tiles

East picks the four tiles (two stacks of two) immediately to the left of the break. The players proceed to take tiles, four at a time, moving left of the break, in the order of East, South, West, and finally North. This is repeated two more times, so that each player has twelve tiles. Then all players draw in turn their thirteenth tile from the wall, and subsequently East draws his fourteenth tile.

East also sees to it that a small break is made between the live and the dead wall, because both walls play their own role in the game. As the game proceeds, players will take turns drawing tiles from the live wall to build their hands, and thus it must be within easy reach of all the players.

Thirteen tiles, unsorted

Now you can have a look at your tiles. Looking at your tiles prematurely, before you have drawn your complete set of starting tiles, is considered impolite. Place your tiles upright like dominoes before you or on your mahjong rack. Take care that the other players cannot see your tiles' faces. You may wish to sort your tiles by their respective types for ease of view, although experienced Chinese players find such ordering superfluous and even advise against it. This is because extremely observant players can make deductions about the nature of a player's hand by carefully watching how the tiles are arranged.

The thirteen tiles are now sorted, with the Circles, Characters, and Bamboos at the left and the Winds and the Dragons at the right.

Tip: It is advisable to vary the manner in which you sort your tiles to keep other players from deducing the locations of the different suits. Taking such precautions will make it nearly impossible for the other players to make reliable conclusions about your hand.

Goal of the Game

The goal of the game is to be the first to make mahjong. You make mahjong by completing four sets of three (or four) tiles and one pair. It is also possible to make mahjong with nonstandard configurations of hands (called special hands), which are composed of elements other than the standard sets. Special hands are discussed in more detail later.

Standard Sets for Hands

The sets are called Chows, Pungs, and Kongs.

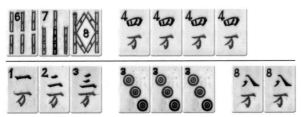

A mahjong hand with one sequence of four tiles, three sequences of three tiles and a pair

Chow

A Chow is a sequence of three consecutive tiles of one suit.

A Chow of Bamboos and a Chow of Characters

Winds and Dragons cannot form Chows.

You can complete a Chow with a tile that you pull from the wall (concealed Chow) or with the tile that your left neighbor discards (melded Chow). When making a melded Chow, you announce "Chow," display your two tiles faceup in front of you on the table, and add the third (discarded) tile to them.

A melded Chow can only be made by a player during her turn.

Though Chows do not score points, they are the basic building block of most hands.

Pung

A Pung is a triplet of three identical tiles.

A Pung of 3-Circles and a Pung of West Winds

You can complete a Pung with a tile that you pull from the wall (concealed Pung), or with a tile that one of the players discards (melded Pung). It does not matter whose turn it is. To declare a melded Pung, you call "Pung," display your two tiles faceup in front of you on the table, and add the third (discarded) tile to them. This Pung is now exposed.

When you complete your Pung with a tile from the wall, it stays concealed on your rack as a concealed Pung. A concealed Pung scores twice as much as an exposed Pung.

Kong

A Kong is a Quad of four identical tiles.

A Kong of 4-Characters and a Kong of Green Dragons

You can make a Kong in three ways:

1. **Melding an exposed Kong.** You have on your rack a concealed Pung and the fourth tile is discarded by another player. You call "Kong," whether it is your turn or not, display your three tiles faceup in front of you on the table, and add the fourth tile to them. This is a melded Kong. Because you are now one tile short of the proper number of tiles to complete your hand, you draw a loose tile from the dead wall.

2. **Melding a concealed Kong.** You have a concealed Pung and pick up the fourth tile from the wall. You now have four identical tiles on your rack, but it only becomes a Kong if it is declared. It is also necessary to draw an extra tile from the dead wall. Display your Kong in front of you on the table with the two middle tiles face down to indicate that this it is concealed. Then draw a loose tile, discard a tile, and proceed to the next player's turn.

A melded and concealed Kong

Tip: It can be tactically advantageous to not declare your Kong immediately to retain more strategic options until a later turn.

Note: In some playing variants, a concealed Kong is put on the table face down so that the Kong stays concealed and the other players don't know which tile is dead.

3. **Upgrading an exposed Pung.** You have an exposed Pung in front of you on the table and you draw the fourth tile from the wall. You are allowed to add

this tile to your Pung, upgrading it to an exposed Kong. Then draw a loose tile, discard a tile, and proceed to the next player's turn. Kongs made in this manner are formed only by tiles drawn from the wall; if the fourth tile of your exposed Pung is discarded by one of the other players, you cannot claim it to make a Kong.

Pair

A pair consists of two identical tiles. A pair can be formed by pulling a tile from the wall or picking up a discarded tile from the table. The latter is allowed only if you complete your hand with this tile.

Drawing and Discarding Tiles

East begins the game by discarding one of his fourteen tiles in the middle of the table, faceup. In addition he calls out the name of that tile. For instance: 2-Bamboo, West Wind, or Red Dragon.

After this, South draws the next tile from the live wall and places it on his or her rack. Next, that player discards the least needed tile, which can also be the tile just drawn. Thus, except for when you draw and discard a fourteenth tile, you hold a hand of thirteen tiles (unless you have declared a Kong). Mahjong is completed with a fourteen-tile hand, and holding thirteen tiles allows you to claim your fourteenth and winning tile from any player's discard. After South comes West, then North, then back to East.

This procedure is only interrupted when one of the players wants to claim a discarded tile to meld a Pung, Kong, or to declare mahjong. Any player may announce one of these actions on any discard. After declaring a Pung or Kong and discarding a fourteenth tile, the player to your right plays next, so that Pung and Kong actions sometimes skip one or two players' turns.

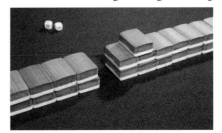

Extra Tile

After declaring a Kong or drawing a bonus tile, you pull the loose tile that is farthest to the end of the the dead wall to

The dead wall is usually replenished with tiles from the end of the live wall so that it always contains fourteen tiles.

replace the missing tile. Each time this happens, a tile from the end of the live wall is added to the dead wall so that it always consists of fourteen tiles, but in some playing variants the dead wall is not replenished, so it becomes shorter with each replacement.

Waiting Hand

A hand that is one tile short of mahjong is called a Waiting Hand. The fourteenth tile may complete one of three elements: a pair, a Pung (Kong), or a Chow. The winning tile may be drawn from the wall or claimed from the last discard on the table.

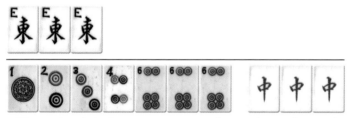

A Waiting Hand. At this point, you are one tile away from mahjong. There are three possibilities: 1-Circles, 4-Circles, and 5-Circles.

When a fourteenth tile completes your hand, you call "mahjong" and expose your hand to the other players. They check to see if you've declared a legitimate mahjong. In some variants, the remaining three players also expose their hands and receive points.

Play then proceeds to the next hand. If East declares mahjong, then he stays East. If one of the other players completes mahjong, then the East seat moves one place over and the former South becomes the new East.

Priority

It can happen that several players are waiting for the same tile. In this case, claiming mahjong has priority over claiming a Pung, a Kong, or a Chow.

If more players want to go mahjong with the same tile, then the following priority rules apply:
* A limit hand (see p. 39) always has priority,
* A pair mahjong has priority over a Pung mahjong, and
* A Pung mahjong has priority over a Chow mahjong.

When the situation is equal for two players, then the player whose turn comes first has priority. When the situation is equal for three players, it is a draw. If priority cannot be determined by the above rules, then the player next in line from the discarded tile takes priority. If three players declare mahjong and priority cannot be determined by the above rules, it is declared a draw and play proceeds to the next hand without scores being settled.

Draw

It will be a draw when the last tile of the live wall is used. No points will be counted. East stays East and the hand will be played again.

End of a Round

A round is complete after all four players have been East once. The next round starts with a new prevailing Wind. In the first round the prevailing Wind is East, for the second round, South, for the third round, West, and the fourth round, North.

East starts each round as leader.

End of the Game

A complete game of mahjong is over when all four Winds have been played.

Limit

Scoring for each mahjong is capped, perhaps because wagers are placed on some games, and an upper limit is necessary to make a game agreeable to all participants. The extent of the limit is agreed upon beforehand. When nothing is stated, a limit of 2000 points applies.

Special Hands

You can also go mahjong with a special hand—a hand so exceptional that it is rewarded with the highest possible score. The composition of the special hands varies among playing variants, and the American playing variant has the greatest number of special hands.

Playing with Bonus Tiles

The seasons and the flowers form the bonus tiles.

The eight bonus tiles aren't used to build hands, but they do increase your score. When you draw a bonus tile, you expose it immediately faceup and pull a replacement tile from the dead wall.

The bonus tiles yield extra points or sometimes double your score. The Winds have two bonus tiles each:

	Season	Flower	Belongs to
1	Spring	Plum	East
2	Summer	Orchid	South
3	Autumn	Chrysanthemum	West
4	Winter	Bamboo	North

When you draw your own bonus tile, then you receive an extra double. And when you have four seasons or four flowers, you get an extra reward: two extra doubles, 1000 points, or the double limit, all depending on the variant you are playing.

Example: When you are West, you will get one double when you draw 3-bonus tile, which is Autumn or Chrysanthemum.

Note: Never forget to draw a loose tile after you expose a bonus tile on the table.

Counting, Doubling, and Settling Scores

To master mahjong it is important to know the value of the sets; otherwise you cannot make good decisions as you build your hand. Counting points is surprisingly simple, although it looks rather complicated at first. Still it takes some time to count the scores, even for experienced players.

The winner receives points from all the players. In the old style of play, the three losers would settle with one another according to their own scores. In the modern form of the game the losers no longer settle among themselves; the winner receives points from one or three players, depending on where the winning tile came from. In some versions, only the doubles are counted. This is done to simplify and speed up the counting.

Settling goes in three steps. First the points are counted, then the points are doubled, and finally the scores are mutually settled.

Counting Points

The tiles themselves have no value. They count only when they have formed a sequence. The only exception is the bonus tiles, since you cannot make sets with them.

When counting points, the tiles can be divided into Simple tiles, Honor and Terminal tiles, and bonus tiles.

The Simples are the tiles numbered 2, 3, 4, 5, 6, 7, and 8 of the three suits. There are eighty-four Simple tiles in total.

Simple tiles

The Honor and Terminal tiles are the Winds and the Dragons plus the 1s and 9s of the three suits. In total, there are fifty-two Honor and Terminal tiles.

The Terminals   *The Honor tiles*

The Terminals are the 1s and 9s of the three suits (twenty-four total tiles) and the Honor tiles are the Winds and Dragons (twenty-eight total tiles).

Points

You score points for the sets of three or four tiles that compose your hand. Simple tiles score relatively few points; and Honors twice as many. Sets of concealed tiles score double the value of the same set of exposed tiles, as shown in the table:

	Concealed	Exposed
Chow	0	0
Pung of Simples	4	2
Pung of Honors and Terminals	8	4
Kong of Simples	16	8
Kong of Honors and Terminals	32	16

These pairs also score points:

Pair of Dragons	2
Pair of prevailing Winds	2
Pair of own Winds	2

Finally, the bonus tiles, which are not used in sets, have point value:

Bonus tile	4

Points Winner

The winner is rewarded with extra points:

Obtaining mahjong	20
Winning tile comes from the wall	2
Winning tile is only possible tile	2
Winning tile completes a pair	2

Only Possible Tile

The definition of Only Possible Tile sometimes causes confusion. It means that there is only one type of tile, and no other that can complete your hand, even if the other tile is no longer available. Here are some examples to illustrate this rule:

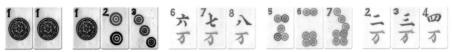

A winning hand. You obtain mahjong with 3-Circles, but you cannot claim Only Possible Tile, because you could also win with 2-Circles, as illustrated in the winning hand below:

Here are some additional examples:

Here 5-Bamboo seems the only possibility, but 3-Bamboo, 4-Bamboo, 6-Bamboo, or 7-Bamboo could also be the winning tile.

Here 4-Circles is the only tile that leads to mahjong and is entitled to 2 points for Only Possible Tile.

Doubling Points

You can earn not only points, but also doubles, which boost your score considerably. For each double, your score is multiplied by a factor of two, such that two doubles quadruples your initial score, three doubles multiples your score by eight, and so on.

1 double	= 2 x points total
2 doubles	= 4 x points total
3 doubles	= 8 x points total
4 doubles	= 16 x points total
5 doubles	= 32 x points total
6 doubles	= 64 x points total
7 doubles	= 128 x points total
8 doubles	= 256 x points total

Each playing variant of mahjong has its own series of doubles for special configurations of tiles. These are the most common (but check before you start playing a variant):

Pung/Kong of Dragons	1 x
Pung/Kong of the prevailing Wind	1 x
Pung/Kong of own Wind	1 x
Three concealed Pungs	1 x
Own Honor tile	1 x
Clean hand (one suit plus Honor tiles)	1 x
Pure hand (one suit only)	3 x
All Chows	1 x
All Pungs	1 x

Two Counting Examples

Counting example 1:

In the South round West obtains mahjong by drawing the West Wind from the wall. The tiles above the line are exposed, the others concealed. This would be his score.

Obtaining mahjong	20
Winning tile comes from the wall	2
Winning tile is only possible tile	2
Winning tiles completes the pair	2
Exposed Kong of 9-Circles	16
Exposed Kong of White Dragons	16
Exposed Pung of South Winds	4

Concealed Pung of 8-Circles	4
Pair of own Winds	2
Own bonus tile	4
Subtotal	72
Doubles:	
Pung of prevailing Winds	1 x
Kong of Dragons	1 x
Clean hand	1 x
All Pungs	1 x
Own bonus tile	1 x

Total 5 x doubling. So that is 2 x 2 x 2 x 2 x 2 = 32 x 72 points = 2304 points

Note: If there is an agreed upon limit of 2,000 points, then West receives 2,000 points from North and South each and 4,000 points from East (who always pays double). So he receives 8,000 points. Not bad!

Counting example 2:

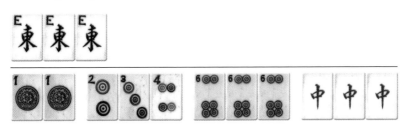

In this example, you are East and go mahjong in the East round with a 1-Circles tile from the wall. It gives you 640 points. Check the scoring:

Obtaining mahjong	20
Winning tile comes from the wall	2
Winning tile completes the pair	2
Exposed Pung of Winds	4
Concealed Pung of 6-Circles	4
Concealed Pung of Dragons	8
Subtotal	40

Doubles:	
Pung of own Winds (East)	1 x
Pung of prevailing Winds	1 x
Pung of Dragons	1 x
Clean hand	1 x
Total 4 doubles = 2 x 2 x 2 x 2 = 16 x 40 points = 640 points	

South has the following hand:

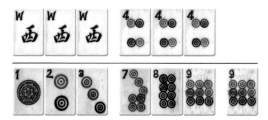

Score of South:

Exposed Pung of Winds	4
Exposed Pung of 4-Circles	2
Concealed Chow of Circles	0
Concealed Chow of Circles	0
Subtotal	6
Doubles:	
Clean hand	1 x
Total 2 x 6 = 12 points	

West has this hand:

Score of West:

Exposed Pung of Dragons	4
Exposed Pung of 9-Characters	4
Concealed Pung of 3-Characters	4
Concealed pair of Dragons	2
Subtotal	14
Doubles:	
Pung of Dragons	1 x
Clean hand	1 x
Total 2 x 2 = 4 x 14 = 56 points	

North has this hand:

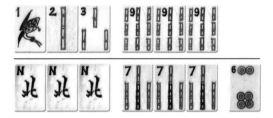

Score of North:

Exposed Chow of Bamboos	0
Exposed Pung of 9-Bamboos	4
Concealed Pung of Winds	8
Concealed Pung of 7-Bamboos	4
Subtotal	16
Doubles:	
Pung of own Wind	1 x
Total 2 x 16 = 32 points	

Settling Points

A friendly characteristic of mahjong is its generosity for losers. Usually they are paid out for their scores. That can be more points than the winner receives. The winner, however, does not have to pay the losers. The losers settle their scores mutually. Only in the most modern variants are losers not paid.

If he wins, the East player receives twice his score from the losers, but if he loses East also has to pay double. Settling is done with the counting sticks.

Settling example 1:
East obtained mahjong and scores 640 points.
South scores 12 points.
West scores 56 points.
North scores 24 points.

That gives the following result:

	Score	Receives	Pays	Total
East (mahjong)	640	1280 + 1280 + 1280	0	+3840
South	12	12 + 12	1280 + 56 + 24	-1336
West	56	56 + 56	1280 + 12 + 24	-1204
North	24	24 + 24	1280 + 12 + 56	-1300

Settling example 2:
West obtained mahjong and scores 68 points.
North scores 24 points.
East scores 12 points.
South scores 6 points.

That leads to the following total scores:

	Score	Receives	Pays	Total
East	12	2 x 12 + 2 x 12	2 x 6 + 2 x 68 + 2 x 24	-148
South	6	2 x 6 + 6	2 x 12 + 24 + 68	-98
West (mahjong)	68	136 + 68 + 68	0	+272
North	24	2 x 24 + 24	2 x 12 + 6 + 68	-26

Although South has the lowest score (6 points), East loses the most points.

Nicknames

If you've ever played mahjong into the wee hours of the morning, you may have found yourself coining personal nicknames for the beautiful and whimsical tiles that kept you fixed to a mahjong table for hours on end. As the mood at the mahjong table sours, the language coarsens and the tiles get the most bizarre nicknames. For example, the mahjong tiles may so stimulate the imagination that you may call 1-Bamboo Woodstock after the feathered friend of the comic hero Snoopy. Here is only a small selection from an abundance of such nicknames that I've heard at many mahjong tables over the years.

1-Circle
Moon, Cake, Pizza, Lid, Dollar

2-Circles
Bike, Glasses, Mr. Magoo

3-Circles
Tricycle, Traffic light

4-Circles
Stove, Rollator

8-Circles
Candy roll, Locomotive, Coffin

9-Circles
Singing choir, Carpetland

1-Bamboo
Bird, Duck, Frog, Woodstock, Chicken

2-Bamboo
Stretcher, Chopping stick, Pole

3-Bamboo
Tripod

4-Bamboo
Table (with four legs)

7-Bamboo
Tank, Puppetshow

8-Bamboo
Fence, Mother Maria, River Kwai

3-Character
Lasagne

4-Character
Teeth

6-Character
Speedy Gonzalez

 7-Character
James Bond

 8-Character
Pi

White Dragon
Soap, Pete (because of the P)

 Green Dragon
Freddy

 Red Dragon
Charley, Cancer stick

 East Wind
Broiler duck

 West Wind
Chopper

OLD CHINA

There has been much conjecture over the age of mahjong and its roots. Some speak of centuries, others of millennia. By rights, some people say mahjong was played by four people in Noah's Ark while it was driven forth by an east wind. In reality, mahjong is only one and a half centuries old. Precursors of the game, however, are quite a bit older. More than twelve hundred years ago, during the Tang dynasty, writers reported that the princess of Chang Kuo was fond of a game called *yehtzu pai,* which centuries later was named *ya pai.* This old game is supposed to be the origin of mahjong. It was played with thirty-two cards made of ivory or wood. The cards look a little bit like mahjong tiles, though their size is more comparable with playing cards. They were called *ku pai,* cards of bone. As time passed, the playing rules changed and the number of cards increased. Five centuries ago it was called *ma tiao* and played with forty cards. There were four suits, one more than nowadays. The cards were numbered from 1 to 9 and there were four bonus cards.

A ma tiao *game from around 1900.*
The cards are made of cardboard.

Chinese playing mahjong, as imagined by an American illustrator

In 1846 the imperial servant Chen Yu-men, an excellent card player and talented diplomat from the harbor city of Ningbo, combined the best elements from *ma tiao* and other card games, replaced the cards with tiles, and thus created mahjong—a new, well-balanced, and challenging game.

The new game became a craze within a few years. The Chinese went gaga over it. The imperial empire was replaced by a republic in 1912 and the new game was exactly the diversion that the Chinese needed in this turbulent time. It became immensely popular. From early in the morning until late at night, from high ranks to low, it was played with passion. A year later the new republic split apart into the North and South, but it did not affect the mahjong craze. In the North as well as in the South the Chinese kept on playing the addictive game passionately. After that China went through more uprisings, disasters, and revolutions, but the Chinese went on imperturbably playing their game of mahjong.

In China, mahjong is as varied as its cuisine—with each region having its own specialties, and each household its own version of familiar recipes. But the game is still as simple as it was prior to the 1920s, when shrewd Western businessmen discovered it and made it famous all over the world. We can look at the rules of this first mahjong game and point out where it differs from the basic mahjong. These rules also reflect how mahjong was played, more or less, before it was introduced to the West.

Seating Arrangements

Before the game can be started, the dice are rolled to decide who will sit where at the table. The rolling of dice is a ritual that is designed to give the supernatural powers control over the course of the game. The Chinese believe that the place where you are seated can be decisive for your luck. This belief is called *feng shui*. The process of selecting the players' seating is therefore not to be taken lightly. If you do it incorrectly, or if you aren't mindful of all regulations, then you can end up at a seat where everything will fail. If you execute the ritual conscientiously and with respect, then your chair can bring you luck and prosperity in your play. The Chinese call that *wong*. The player whose chair is wong will succeed in everything. He can neglect discarded tiles and trust that he will draw all his wanted tiles from the wall.

He can risk everything and still win constantly, first with small victories but later on even with special hands. How long your chair is wong depends on the whims of the ghosts, but a whole evening is not unusual.

So it is wise to execute the opening ceremony carefully and to accept the will of the dice. Through the dice, the ghosts let you know in which order the four players have to be seated around the table, which chair is for East, and who may start the game as the East Wind.

To begin, the players take places at the table in random order. One of them throws two dice. It does not matter whom, but it is polite to let your host do it. Then, starting with himself, he counts counterclockwise the total of the thrown eyes. In this way the indicated player becomes "temporary East."

Now the four Wind tiles—East, South, West, and North—are put on the table facedown, mixed, and arranged in a line. As shown below, the line is closed on the one side with an even-numbered exposed tile and on the other side with an odd-numbered exposed tile.

Temporary East now throws the two dice and counts, beginning with himself, the total of the thrown eyes counterclockwise. In this way he indicates the player who is allowed to be the first to draw a Wind tile. If the total is even, than this player has to pick up the blind Wind tile at the even end of the line; if the total is odd, then he picks up the Wind tile at the odd end.

Now the rest of the players each draw the next Wind tiles. In this way they each get assigned a Wind, which designates their position around the table. The player who drew East is seated on the chair that is assigned for East. At this moment the mutual order is decided. The player who drew the East Wind decides hereafter who will become final East and start the game. He throws the dice and starting with himself, he counts counterclockwise the total of the thrown eyes, to indicate the final East Wind. The player right of East becomes South, the next player West, and the other player North.

Example: Colonel Qin Lan invited you to his house to play the Game of the Hundred Wonders together with the enchanting Li (Plum blossom) and the beautiful Li-en (Lotus). After the exchange of pleasantries you seat yourselves around the mahjong table. Your host insists that you are seated at his right side. Li is sitting to the left of the colonel and Li-en to the right of you.

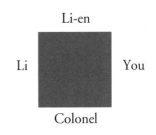

Li-en

Li   You

Colonel

Courteously you give the two dice to your host. The colonel throws 6. He counts up (counterclockwise) himself, you, Li-en, Li, himself, you. So you become "temporary East."

Li has already put the four Wind tiles on the table facedown—East, South, West, and North—mixed them, and laid them in a line with an even-numbered tile on one side and an odd-numbered tile on the other.

Now you cast the two dice, throw 10, and count the players counterclockwise according to that number. You are 1, 5, and 9, so the next temporary East is Li-en, the beautiful lady who sits to the right of you.

Because it is an even throw, Li-en picks up the Wind tile at the even side of the row. It is West. Li draws the next tile: East. After that, the colonel picks up North and Li-en finally South. You have now decided on the mutual order and place yourself at the table in this order.

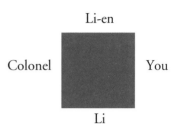

Li, who has drawn the East Wind, will now decide with the two dice who may start the game. That player will be the final East. She throws 10 and points to you. The temporary names are no longer used. You become East, Li South, the colonel West, and Li-en North.

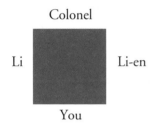

Scoring Sticks

Every player gets 29 sticks with a total value of 2000 points.

2 sticks of 500	= 1000 points
9 sticks of 100	= 900 points
8 sticks of 10	= 80 points
10 sticks of 2	= 20 points

Building the Wall

The bonus tiles do not participate and are removed from the set. There are 136 tiles in total. The walls are 17 tiles long and 2 tiles high.

Breaking the Wall

Break the wall as described in chapter 2. In theory, every player can make four Kongs, sixteen in total. Therefore the dead wall will have sixteen extra tiles, which is why it is also called the Kong box. The dead wall is not replenished when a tile is taken from it.

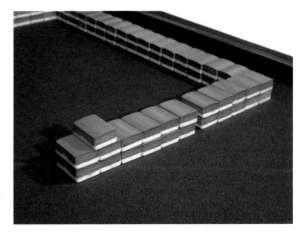

The tiles of the dead wall are not replenished.

The rest of the game is played like basic mahjong (see chapter 2).

Doubling Points

If the winner has succeeded in creating beautiful or notable special sequences or in winning in an exceptional way, then he or she will be rewarded with extra doubles of the scored points. This applies in the following cases, for which the Chinese have devised some very poetic names:

All Chows	1 x double	Four chows and a pair
All Pungs	1 x double	A hand without chows
Concealed hand	1 x double	Your hand is concealed and you have drawn all the tiles from the wall, including the last, winning tile.
Clean hand	1 x double	You have tiles of only one suit and Honor tiles.
Pure hand	3 x double	You have tiles of only one suit.
All Honors and Terminals	1 x double	You have only Dragons, Winds, 1s, and 9s.
All Honors	2 x double	You have only Winds and/or Dragons.
Winning from the Roof	1 x double	You win with a loose tile from the dead wall.
Winning from the Bottom of the Sea	1 x double	You win with the last tile from the live wall, which is also the last tile before a draw.

Catching the Fish from the Bottom of the River	1 x double	You win with the last discarded tile, at the very last moment before a draw.
The Happy Thirteen	1 x double	You win with 13 original tiles from the start of the game plus a winning tile. You are not allowed to discard your original tiles, only the tile you pull from the wall at the time. You should announce this hand at the start.
Robbing a Kong	1 x double	One of the players pulls a tile from the wall to promote an exposed Pung to an exposed Kong. If you can win with this tile, you are allowed to rob it. The robbed player may only count his Pung, but you receive an extra double.

Limit

Because the Chinese like to stake money in the game of mahjong, a limit applies to the points that you can win with a hand. The height of that limit is agreed upon before the game. If nothing different is agreed upon, then a limit of 1000 points applies.

Special Hands

The Chinese game of mahjong recognizes eight special hands. They are highly valued and are rewarded with the maximum score. Chinese special hands are regular hands that are formed according to the playing rules. They are very rare and almost impossible to obtain.

Heaven's Blessing

East's first hand, received immediately after the distribution of the tiles, is a winning hand, considered blessed by heaven.

Earth's Blessing

Immediately after the distribution of the tiles South, North, or West has a ready hand and wins with East's first discard.

Gathering the Plum Blossom from the Roof

Winning with a loose tile from the dead wall and that loose tile happens to be 5-Circles (which to the Chinese resembles the blossoms of a plum tree).

Plucking the Moon from the Bottom of the Sea

If the last tile of the live wall is a 1-Circle, and you declare mahjong by picking this tile, you are Plucking the Moon from the Bottom of the Sea. Winning with the last tile from the wall, "from the bottom of the sea," is already honored with one double, but if you pluck 1-Circles, "the moon," then this surprise is rewarded with the maximum score.

Scratching a Carrying Pole

You win by robbing a Kong of 2-Bamboo, which looks a little bit like a "carrying pole."

Twofold Fortune

You declare a Kong, pull a loose tile, and complete a second Kong with it, after which you pull a second loose tile that proves to be your winning tile. This special occasion is also called "Kong on Kong."

Fourfold Plenty

You win with a hand of four Kongs and a pair. The Kongs may be exposed or concealed and the pair can be of any tile.

Concealed Treasure

You win with a hand of four Pungs and a pair, completely concealed. A Kong, exposed or concealed, counts as a concealed Pung.

Mahjong Makes History

At the beginning of the last century the Chinese trade port Shanghai was known as "Paris of the East" or more derogatorily as "the whore of Asia." After the first Opium War (1839–1842), the British were able to dictate that the city would be unlocked for unlimited western free trade, enabling them to make use of the dirt cheap Chinese labor forces. French, Italians, Germans, and Americans followed greedily in the track of the British. The foreigners changed the city into a merry-go-round of amusement and decay. The western enclave was forbidden for "Chinese and dogs" and because strangers fell outside the Chinese laws they could do whatever they liked. Morals didn't matter. Shanghai became synonymous with licentiousness and lawlessness. Uninhibited prostitution, crime, and opium addiction characterized the city. All foreigners longed for a fast fortune in trade or at the gambling tables.

The wall is symbolic of the closed Chinese society to which Europeans were hardly admitted. However, a wall could not stop the British and French troops who, in 1860, fought their way through Peking's protective wall to force diplomatic relations in terms of equality.

One of the foreign fortune hunters was the American Joseph Park Babcock, a representative of Standard Oil. When, in one of the smoky gambling dens, he was introduced to the game that had China under its spell, he understood immediately that a fortune could be made by exporting the mahjong craze to America. Babcock proceeded cautiously and deliberately. He supposed that some adjustments to the game had to be made to make it irresistible to his fellow Americans. He knew that the game should be easy to understand and play. Therefore Babcock had Western numbers placed on the mahjong tiles, simplified the rules, deleted all special hands, and invented mahjong racks to facilitate the playing. In September 1920 he shipped the first mahjong sets to the United States. Within two years mahjong was a smash hit in America.

Mounted in nice oak, rosewood, or lacquer drawers, and studded with copper or nickel, the sets flew out of the shops in record time. The prices varied from $18 to $34. That was much more than one had to pay for a deck of cards, but Americans

Joseph P. Babcock made mahjong popular in America.

didn't care. It was the Roaring Twenties and the Americans fell eagerly upon every new kind of amusement. In 1907 it was the Diablo that carried away the American people, in 1913 Ping-Pong, but the mahjong madness of 1923 surpassed everything. That year mahjong became Shanghai's number five export, with a turnover of $1,505,000. The Chinese laborers could hardly keep up with the demand and the Chinese cows even less. Shiploads of bones from American slaughterhouses were sailed to China with the plea to return them as soon as possible in the form of mahjong sets.

It was not only the sets that attracted the American public but also everything associated with them. Magazine articles about the tactics, background, and especially about the history of the exotic game were devoured. In China they play mahjong with a square hole in the middle of the table, one author alleged. The discarded tiles disappear in the hole, so that the players are forced to use mental recall. According to the article, a servant sits under the table to catch the tiles and to place them back on the table as soon as a game is over.

Americans couldn't get enough of these stories. Debate about the age of the game kept many writers busy, and many publications were devoted to this intriguing question. One writer claimed that the game was already played during the reign of the first Chinese emperor Qin Shi Huangdi, who governed from 221–209 B.C.E., and who started the construction of the Chinese wall. Thus, he proposed, the practice of building a wall of tiles at the beginning of each mahjong game was done out of respect for this ruler.

Another writer declared he had traced down the exact year the game was invented—472 B.C.E.—but forgot to inform his audience how he calculated his discovery. According to the story, a princess in the court of King Wu invented the game to drive away the miserable weariness in the palace. The game that was played with ivory cards became very popular with the court ladies and bore the name of *"Pe-ling."*

Nevertheless most "experts" agreed that the famous Chinese philosopher Confucius invented the game in the sixth century B.C.E. Confucius traveled with his disciples through the country to preach his ideas. According to the American experts he took the opportunity to also promote his mahjong game. As proof for this curious thesis they mentioned that the three Dragons in the game, *Chung, Fa,* and *Po,* correspond with the three main thoughts of Confucius: benevolence, sincerity, and devoutness. Moreover Confucius was fond of birds, which is why he supposedly called mahjong the "game of the sparrows," his Chinese name sounded like *Kong Fuzi* (master Kong), and he was married to a girl with the name of *Che* or *Chow*.

Yet another historian dated the birth of mahjong even further back. Three thousand years ago there was a simple fisherman by the name of Sze. He thought to himself that he could catch more fish if he threw his nets, not along the shore, but out at sea. He recruited a hundred fishermen to test his new method and sailed out to sea with them. Everything went well until the wind came up and, to the fearful landlubbers, everything around them seemed to move. They became seasick and had to be brought ashore. But according to the counselor of the Sze family the seasickness was only in the mind of the fishermen. So when Sze wanted to continue his bizarre experiment he had to make sure that his fishermen's thoughts were not with the heaving sea but with something else. Sze went into a long and serious brainstorming session with his nine brothers. The result of this deliberation was the game *ma tiau,* which soon had the fishermen so much under its spell that they could not think about anything else. The seasickness disappeared and the game of mahjong was born.

According to one theory, the Chinese philosopher Confucius invented and promoted the game of mahjong in the sixth century B.C.E.

Another writer pointed to the biblical character Noah as the first mahjong player. He and his three sons played mahjong in the Ark for forty days and nights. This theory was based on two odd facts: the Ark was pushed by the eastern wind and the east wind plays an important role in mahjong. The animals came into the Ark two by two. Thus "two by two" or "seven pairs" is a popular special hand in the game, according to this author. How it was possible to play in the Ark with only one opening that was very small, according to Genesis 6, was not explained by him.

Americans indulged in fantasy not only about the history but also about the rules. Babcock had simplified the rules. The mahjong fever stimulated others to make the game more complicated and more exciting. They invented all kinds of ways to raise the score, because Americans love records and huge numbers. One way to score more points is to make it more difficult to get mahjong because in this way players have more chance to create richer combinations and get more points. So the One Double Rule was invented: one is only allowed to go out when he or she has at least one doubling of his score. Another American invention was the Cleared-Hand Rule: a player can only go out when he or she has only tiles of one suit with or without Honors.

These small changes had big consequences. The nature of the game changed and, in some cases, the Game of the Thousand Possibilities was reduced to bingo level, meaning that you simply win when you are the first to draw all the right tiles. The players were forced first to throw away their "rubbish" before they could taste the excitement of winning. But they were rewarded with impressive scores and had the impression they had become excellent mahjong players.

More ideas were thought of to raise the score. With great inventiveness, new Doublings and new special hands were created with exotic names like Gertie's Garter, Heavenly Twins, and Yin Yang. There were no boundaries in raising the scores and even a bizarre reward of "double limit" came into existence for hands like "Christmas" or "Royal Ruby." Every self-respecting mahjong club—there were hundreds of them—did its best to distinguish itself with its own special hands and with a ban on the special hands of others.

Very soon there were more rules than mahjong tiles. Everybody followed different rules and you could only start to play after long and in-depth explanations of them. The fun was fast over. By the end of the 1920s, the mahjong craze had died. The importation of mahjong sets stopped as suddenly as it started. The importers were stuck with supplies of mahjong sets, worth about two million dollars. The Americans turned to another rage: miniature golf.

A street scene from 1913 showing a European couple doing their shopping in Shanghai. Thanks to the cheap labor in China, Europeans were able to live a life of luxury.

AMERICA

Though the American mahjong craze ended with the close of the Roaring Twenties, not every American switched from playing mahjong to the next faddish entertainment—miniature golf. Many people stayed loyal to mahjong and taught the game to their children and grandchildren. More recently, others have come under its spell via the Internet, where it is presently prominent. The exoticism of the tiles and their intriguing names has not lost its attraction in the digital era. On the contrary, mahjong is still played a lot in the United States. The 1920s explosion of rules and variants can still be seen in how the game is played today. In the country of unlimited possibilities, mahjong is played in roughly three manners:

- All-American mahjong,
- Maj,
- Military mahjong.

Most Americans play the All-American variant.

In the 1920s the song "Since Ma Is Playing Mah Jong," written by Bill Rose and Con Conrad, was a smash hit in the United States. Eddie Cantor sang it in the musical Kid Boots.

All-American

When comparing the All-American playing manner with the basic rules, the following differences are striking:

- An exchange of unwanted tiles at the start of the game, called the Charleston;
- More tiles, because the bonus tiles participate;
- No dead wall;
- A very large number of special hands;
- A distinct idiom.

The attractive drawer boxes from the time of Joseph Babcock made way for dull synthetic cases, which have the habit of tearing after a certain time and getting loose handles. Stains, however, are long-lasting. An American mahjong set weighs a little more than a Chinese set, which has 136 tiles. Standard American sets have 144 tiles, plus eight Jokers for a total of 152 tiles; however, you may find American sets with numerous bonus tiles and no Jokers.

Seating Arrangements

The allocation of seats at the table is done with four different Wind tiles, which are laid facedown on the table and then mixed well. The four players draw a Wind tile to decide who sits where around the table.

The four players can also throw two dice and let the number rolled determine the seats. The player with the highest throw becomes East, the runner up becomes South, and so on.

Breaking the Wall—American-Style

In old China there is a long, drawn-out ritual for breaking the wall that you must follow before you can begin to play. In America a much shorter—and so much faster—procedure was developed. The wall has four sides of eighteen tiles. East throws two dice. The number of eyes determines which wall will be broken and where.

- East opens his wall after a roll of 5 or 9;
- South opens his wall after a roll of 2, 6, or 10;
- West opens his wall after a roll of 3, 7, or 11; and
- North opens his wall after a roll of 4, 8, or 12.

The dice-appointed player counts the number rolled from right to left and breaks the wall there. He takes the two tiles from that end of the wall and places them on top of the tail end of the wall, at the right side of the gap. These two tiles mark the dead wall, or flower wall, as Americans prefer to say.

Example: East rolls a 7. He counts the players counterclockwise: East, South, West, North, East, South, and West. The wall of West must be broken. Therefore West counts seven tiles into his wall, from his right to left. The wall is broken between the seventh and eighth tiles (counted along the top of the wall, such that exactly fourteen tiles are left to the right of the break). He takes the two tiles from the tail end of the wall (immediately right of the break) and places them on the flower wall just right of the break. Then East, the first player to act, begins taking tiles.

Optional: When East throws a double, that hand is played for double the points. All players now double their wins and losses.

The flower wall always consists of fourteen tiles and is replenished after each bonus tile and Kong. In the American game, an invisible mystery guest participates in the game behind the dead wall with as many tiles as East. This mystery guest decides your luck. Therefore it is important to treat the dead wall decently and replenish it so that it always has fourteen tiles.

American young ladies, dressed in the fashion of the Roaring Twenties, throw the dice at the beginning of their game of mahjong.

Nowadays American mahjong is played without a flower wall because replenishing is a troublesome delay. You play until the whole wall is exhausted and all the tiles are gone. This also has the advantage of increasing the time it takes to reach a draw and of increasing the amount that can be scored. When the game reaches the flower wall, then the loose tiles are placed back at their original spot on the end of the wall. These become the last tiles that can be drawn. If all tiles are drawn and no player has finished, that hand is a draw.

Mahjong Racks

American mahjong racks have four pins on which players can place their chips, keeping them in good order. The Americans don't play with the elongated sticks but with brightly colored plastic coins that have a hole in the middle.

The player whose wall has been broken has to place his wall so that it is within easy reach of the other players and therefore he pushes it oblique to the middle. If his wall is exhausted, then the next player pushes her wall oblique to the middle, so that everyone can pick up the tiles easily.

Chips

You get 1,000 points in coins. These chips stand on your pins:

4 chips of	200	= 800
6 chips of	25	= 150
10 chips of	5	= 50

Charleston

Before starting the real game you must first do the Charleston! Named after that popular American dance of the 1920s, the Charleston requires a mutual exchange of tiles. This step is obligatory. Even if you don't have a single tile you want to lose, and even when you have a mahjong on your rack, you have to participate in the Charleston.

Each player slides three tiles facedown to his right neighbor: East to South, South to West, and so on. The players look at the new tiles and next slide three tiles toward their opposite neighbor: East to West, South to North, and so on. Again the players judge their hands. Now three tiles have to be passed to the left neighbor. But now when you decide that your hand has enough chances to win, you may push one or two tiles to your left neighbor. East pushes to North, South to East, and so on.

Free Charleston (Optional)
After the obliged Charleston, a free Charleston is possible when all four players are in favor. If there is an objection of one or more players, then this "dance" is canceled. The free Charleston develops the same way as the obliged Charleston and has to be finished completely.

After the Charleston is finished, the players have the same number of

Four young American women patiently pose with their new love—mahjong. The Chinese game was a craze in America during the 1920s.

tiles as they did when they started, but probably a better chance for a good game—plus some insight in the intentions of the other players. It is very unusual not to have a great group of tiles on your rack after doing a free Charleston.

Ding Dong

During the game East (and only East) can demand an exchange of tiles on a smaller scale: the Ding Dong. At East's request, and at a moment she likes, all players push an undesirable tile facedown to the others: one to the left, one to the opposite, and one to the right. East is entitled to repeat this procedure two times more during the game, three times in total.

Kitty

At this point your hand may be so cleaned out that you long to start the real game. Sorry. First everyone has to donate a contribution of 100 points to the pot, called the "kitty." If doubles are thrown at the start of the game when breaking the wall, then the donation to the kitty is 200 points. The contents of the kitty goes to the player who makes a Pung (or Kong) mahjong. If that does not happen then the kitty is not paid out and the players donate again 100 (or 200) points to the pot. The content of the kitty can rise quite high.

Discarding

Now the game can finally start. East discards a tile and calls "Two Cracks." This is not a request for drugs, but an idiom for 2-Character. Americans love short words, their tongues stumble over words like Character, and therefore they have invented shortcuts that sound like gunshots in Westerns. Bam! Crack! Dots! "Bam" is a shortcut for Bamboo, "Crack" for Characters, and "Dots" for Circles.

Optional: To make the game more difficult the discarded tiles can be put blind at the table, that is, with their faces down. Cribbing at the table will then be impossible.

Sweep

The first person to Pung or Kong using East's discarded tile receives 2 extra points. This is called a Sweep or also a Blitz. One of the tiles of the exposed Pung or Kong is laid crosswise to remind everyone that the 2 extra points need to be settled at the end of the game.

Harder Mahjong

In the 1920s, when the game was introduced by Joseph Babcock, many Americans found his rules too simple. According to the Babcock rules, you could go out with any four sequences and a pair. Two different games were invented to replace Babcock's mixed-hand game: the Cleared-Hand game and the One-Double game. They made going out more difficult and increased the average score. Both rules allow players to create more beautiful hands.

Cleared-Hand Game

You may only go out when you have a Cleared-Hand; that is, a hand of only tiles of one suit with or without Honor tiles, or only Terminal tiles with or without Honor tiles.

Under the Cleared-Hand rule this hand, which holds only tiles of one suit with Honor tiles, can go mahjong.

One-Double Game

You may only go out with a hand that scores at least one Double, exclusive of bonus tiles.

This hand holds a Pung of Dragons, which counts as one Double, and thus may be proclaimed as mahjong under the One-Double rule.

Both the Cleared-Hand and the One-Double rules are very popular because they guarantee impressive points totals. These rules greatly raise the scores and give the impression of a miraculous play. However, there is some bad with the good: a consequence of these rules is that the game has become duller and, for the most part, players dump their dirty tiles—that is, tiles that are not a good fit and hence spoil their "clean" hand.

In the All-American mahjong, as it is played today, you can only go out with a clear hand containing no more than one Chow. No mixed suits are allowed.

Goulash (Optional)

A Goulash is when the game ends in a draw and the hand is replayed. If the live wall and the flower wall are totally exhausted and no one has obtained mahjong, players can opt for a Goulash. During a Goulash, each player donates 100 more points to the kitty and starts the game again. The players' Winds do not rotate, which means East stays East, and so on. After the Goulash the Wind always passes, East becomes North, even if he won. Goulash is especially popular with Australians.

Another variation of the Goulash is to play for the entire kitty, not for points. When doing this, each player donates the half limit to the pot. Only one Charleston is permitted and Chows are not allowed, so that it is more difficult to go out. Whoever obtains mahjong wins the pot.

Settling Points

The points you score in the All-American are the same as in basic mahjong.

	Concealed	Exposed
Chow	0	0
Pung of Simple tiles	4	2
Pung of Honors	8	4
Kong of Simple tiles	16	8
Kong of Honors	32	16
Pair of Dragons	2	2
Pair of prevailing Winds	2	2
Pair of own Winds	2	2
Pair of Winds	2	2
Pair of Terminals	2	2
Pung, Kong, or Chow with East's first discard		2
Going mahjong	20	20

Flowers and Seasons

The bonus tiles are also used. They are mostly called flowers and seasons. When you draw a bonus tile, you expose it immediately and pull a substitute tile from the flower wall. The bonus tiles give extra points and, when you are lucky enough to pick the bonus tile belonging to your Wind, you receive an extra double:

Each flower or season tile	4 points
Own flower or season tile	1 double
Flower or season tile of the round	1 double
All flowers or all seasons	1000 points

Doubles for All Players

The All-American rules are generous with doubles. Even the losers get some doubles:

1 x Double

- Pung/Kong of Dragons,
- Pung/Kong of prevailing Wind,
- Pung/Kong of own Wind, and
- Cleared-Hand (one suit with Honors or Terminals with Honors).

3 x Double

- Pure hand: only one suit.

Doubles for the Winner

The winner may claim still more doubles for an exceptional hand and/or for the exceptional way he places his winning tile.

The winning tile is rewarded extra in the following four hands, which are regarded as exceptional:

Concealed Hand

When your hand is concealed and your winning tile is a discarded tile, you get 1 double.

Fully Concealed Hand

When your hand is concealed and you draw the winning tile from the wall, you get a second double.

Winning with the last tile of the wall is called "Winning from the Bottom of the Sea."

You win with the last tile of the wall, before it becomes a draw. You have to draw the tile yourself. It counts as 1 double.

Robbing a Kong

One of the players pulls a tile from the wall with which he can promote an exposed Pung to a Kong. If you can go out with that tile, you may rob that tile. Robbing a Kong realizes 1 double.

South

West

South draws 2-Circles from the wall and uses it to promote his exposed Pung to a Kong. However, West can obtain mahjong with 2-Circles and so claims 2-Circles. This robbery gives him 1 extra double.

Note: Robbing the Kong is a rare but also an exciting event. Imagine requiring a tile, but seeing it already locked in an exposed Pung. There is only one tile left for you to complete your hand, and you do not even know if it is still live or being used by another player. And then, by a stroke of luck, the player who holds the Pung of the needed tile draws the fourth and final tile, and moreover, decides to declare a Kong with it! You finish your hand, with the added rare bonus of Robbing the Kong!

Doubles for Special Hands

America is the land of abundance, as evinced by the number of special hands. It is also the country of unlimited possibilities. With some special hands you can even win a double limit. The limit is 500 points, double limit 1000 points. Americans recognize the six classic hands, as well as their own native-grown hands.

Classic Hands

Here are the American classic hands.

Four Kongs

The Kongs can be concealed or exposed and the pair is completely arbitrary. Score: limit.

Three Dragons

A hand with three Pungs or Kongs of Dragons, exposed or concealed. This special hand is also called *Three Great Scholars*.
Score: limit.

Four Winds

Four Pungs or Kongs of Winds and any pair. It may be played exposed. This special hand is also called *Four Blessings*.
Score: double limit.

All Honors
A hand containing only Honor tiles. It may be played exposed.
Score: limit.

Heads and Tails
A hand containing only Terminals. It may be played exposed.
Score: limit.

Thirteen Orphans

One each of all Honors and Terminals plus one tile double. It may be played exposed. This special hand is also called *Thirteen Unique Wonders*.
Score: limit.

Special Hands

American inventiveness was used in devising special hands. At first all kinds of special relations between the tiles were discovered. Suddenly there appeared to be "Green Bamboos." These are the Bamboo tiles on which (mostly) no red color is used: 2-, 3-, 4-, 6-, and 8-Bamboo. Also the Green Dragon was proclaimed to be a "green tile," so that a mahjong set nowadays has six "green tiles" at its disposal.

Note: In many mahjong sets 3-Bamboo is not completely green; the middle Bamboo is often colored red. Despite that, this tile counts as "green tile."

The Green Bamboos and the Green Dragons are called the "green tiles."

The Bamboo tiles with some red paint on them, with the exception of 3-Bamboo, are called the "Red Bamboos." These are 1-, 5-, 7-, and 9-Bamboo.

The Red Bamboo tiles

Additional "red tiles" were invented. These are the Red Dragon and the 2-, 3-, 4-, 6-, and 8-Characters. They don't look redder than the other Character tiles, but they are the counterparts of the "green tiles." Don't mix them up with the "Red Bamboo" tiles.

The Red Characters and the Red Dragon together are called the "red tiles."

And finally among the Circle tiles there is also a special kind of tile: the "Green Circles." Again these are the 2-, 3-, 4-, 6-, and 8-Circles.

The Green Circles

Ruby Hand

Four Pungs/Kongs of exclusively Red Bamboos and a pair of Red Dragons.
It can be played exposed.
Score: limit.

Jade Hand
Four combinations of only Green Bamboos plus a pair of Green Dragons.
It can be played exposed.
Score: limit.

Pearl Hand
Four combinations of only Green Circles plus a pair of White Dragons.
It can be played exposed.
Score: limit.

Imperial Jade
A Pung/Kong of Green Dragons, three Pungs/Kongs/Chow, and a pair, all of
which are Green Bamboos. Only one Chow permitted.
It can be played exposed.
Score: double limit.

Imperial Pearl
A Pung/Kong of White Dragons, three Pungs/Kongs/Chows, and a pair, all of
which are Green Circles. Only one Chow permitted.
It can be played exposed.
Score: double limit.

Imperial Ruby
A Pung/Kong of Red Dragons, three Pungs/Kongs/Chows, and a pair, all of which are Red Characters. Only one Chow permitted.
It can be played exposed.
Score: double limit.

Ruby Jade
A Pung/Kong of Red Dragons, a Pung/Kong of Green Dragons, a Pung/Kong of Green Bamboos, a Pung/Kong of Red Bamboos, and a pair of Bamboos.
It can be played exposed.
Score: limit.

All Red
Only red tiles.
It can be played exposed.
Score: limit.

The Dragons have additional relatives. The Green Dragon is coupled to the Bamboos, the Red Dragon to the Characters, and the White Dragon to the Circles.

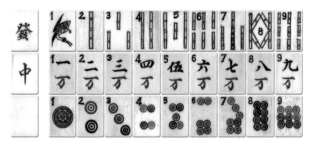

The three Dragons and their related families

These special hands have this family relation:

Golden Gate
A Pung of 1s or 9s, pair of 2-, 4-, 6-, 8-tiles, all of one suit, plus a Pung of related Dragons.

The hand has to be concealed, except for the winning tile.
Score: limit.

Dragon Gates
A Pung of 1s or 9s, tiles 2 through 8, one Simple tile Double, all of one suit, plus a Pung of related Dragons.
The hand has to be concealed, except for the winning tile.
Score: limit.

There are also gates without related Dragons:

Simple Gates
A Pung of 1s, tiles 2 through 8, a Pung of 9s, and one Simple tile Double, all of one suit.
The hand has to be concealed, except for the winning tile.
Score: half limit.

Confused Gates
A Pung of 1s in one suit, tiles 2 through 8 of another suit, a Pung of 9s in the third suit, and one Simple tile Double.
The hand has to be concealed, except for the winning tile.
Score: limit.

True Gates
A Pung of 1s, pairs of 2-, 4-, 6-, 8-tiles, a Pung of 9s, all of one suit.
The hand has to be concealed, except for the winning tile.
Score: limit.

NEWS
The mahjong tiles proved to have their own NEWS-group. Although the playing direction is E-S-W-N, Americans like to arrange the letters so that they spell out the word *news*.

The NEWS-group

This invention inspired several new special hands, including:

Chop Suey

Chows 1-2-3 of each suit, NEWS, plus one Wind Double.
The hand has to be concealed, except for the winning tile.
Score: limit.

Sukiyaki

Chows 4-5-6 of each suit, NEWS, plus one Wind Double.
The hand has to be concealed, except for the winning tile.
Score: limit.

Chow Mein

Chows 7-8-9 of each suit, NEWS, plus one Wind Double.
The hand has to be concealed, except for the winning tile.
Score: limit.

Lil

Chow 1-2-3 of one suit, Chow 4-5-6 of second suit, Chow 7-8-9 of third suit,
NEWS, plus Wind Double.
The hand has to be concealed, except for the winning tile.
Score: limit.

Gone With the Wind

Three times NEWS (in other words, four Pungs of all Winds) and a pair of
Dragons.

This hand can be played exposed.
Score: double limit.

Note: You can also call this hand *Four Winds,* which gives the same reward but sounds less romantic.

Suit Pairs and Honor Orphans

Five pairs of one suit plus the three Dragons and one tile Double; or five pairs plus all the Wind tiles; or NEWS.
The hand has to be concealed, except for the winning tile.
Score: limit.

Down You Go

Four 2-tiles, three 3-tiles, two 6-tiles, one 8-tile of one suit, plus NEWS.
The hand has to be concealed, except for the winning tile.
Score: double limit.

Up You Go

One 2-tile, two 4-tiles, three 6-tiles, four 8-tiles of one suit, plus NEWS.
The hand has to be concealed, except for the winning tile.
Score: double limit.

Windy Chows

One Chow of each suit, NEWS, and one tile Double.
The hand has to be concealed, except for the winning tile.
Score: half limit.

Still more special hands were born through the invention of the twins and the serpents.

The twins are pairs of two identical tiles. Seven twins make a mahjong. All pairs have to be played concealed, except the winning tile. In five special cases you score the limit.

Seven Pairs

Seven pairs	Seven arbitrary pairs	half limit
All Honor pairs	Only Honor tiles	limit
All Terminal pairs	Only Terminal pairs	limit
All Honor and Terminal pairs	Only Honor and Terminal pairs	limit
Cleared pairs	Only one suit and Honor pairs	limit
Pure pairs	Only one suit	limit

Pure Pairs

Serpents

A serpent is a special hand with a sequence of successive tiles, mostly the tiles 1 through 9 (also called "street"), but also a sequence from 1 to 7 (known as a "short street").

Peking Garden

Tiles 1 through 7 of one suit, all Winds, all Dragons.
This hand has to be concealed, except for the winning tile.
Score: limit.

Dragon's Tail

Tiles 1 through 9 of one suit and/or a Pung/Kong of Dragons and pair of Winds, or a Pung/Kong of Winds and a pair of Dragons.
Score: half limit with exposed combination(s); limit when fully concealed.

Run, Pung, and Pair

Tiles 1 through 9, a Pung, and a pair, all of one suit.
Except for the winning tile, this hand has to be concealed.
Score: limit.

Wriggling Snake

Tiles 1 through 9 of one suit, all Winds, one tile Double.
This hand has to be concealed, except for the winning tile.
Score: limit.

Five Odd Honors

Tiles 1 through 9 of one suit, five different Honors.
This hand has to be concealed, except for the winning tile.
Score: limit.

Knitting

Only two suits, each tile paired with the same number of the other suit.
The hand has to be concealed, except for the winning tile.
Score: half limit.

Double Knitting

With "double knitting," even more possibilities for new special hands were created. Double knits match equal numbered tiles—2-Bamboo to 2-Character, for instance. There are also triple knits: 2-Bamboo, 2-Character, and 2-Circles, for instance.

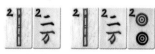

Double knit   *Triple knit*

Gertie's Garter

The tiles 1 through 7 double knitted with two suits.
The hand has to be concealed, except for the winning tile.
Score: limit.

Triple Knitting

Four combinations of one of each suit with same number, plus a knitted pair.
The hand has to be concealed, except for the winning tile.
Score: half limit.

Numbers and Anniversaries

The numbers and the anniversaries are American inventions that produce very special hands that all score a double limit.

Number Rackets

Three Pungs/Kongs of three suits and same number, a Pung/Kong of Dragons, and a pair of Dragons.
The hand has to be concealed, except for the winning tile.
Score: double limit.

Double Numbers

Four Pungs/Kongs of two suits and two same numbers, and a pair of Winds or Dragons.
The hand has to be concealed, except for the winning tile.
Score: double limit.

Christmas

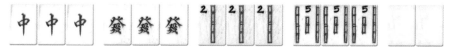

A Pung of Red Dragons, a Pung of Green Dragons, a Pung of 2-tiles, a Pung of 5-tiles of one suit, and a pair of White Dragons. This hand gets its name from the red and green of the Christmas holiday and from the pair of White Dragons that to some look like a small topping of white snow.

This hand can be played exposed.

Score: double limit.

Civil War

Tiles 1-8-6-1 of one suit, tiles 1-8-6-5 of another suit, Pung of North Winds, and a Pung of South Winds. The American Civil War between the North and the South lasted from 1861–1865.

The hand has to be concealed, except for the winning tile.

Score: double limit.

Hong Kong

Tiles 1-8-4-2 of one suit, tiles 1-9-9-7 of another suit, a Pung of East Winds, and a Pung of West Winds.

The hand has to be concealed, except for the winning tile. Hong Kong was a Western crown colony in the Far East from 1842 until 1997.

Score: double limit.

Maj

In 1937 a group of players in New York founded the National Mah Jongg League to stop the proliferation of playing rules, which had made mahjong in America unnecessarily difficult to play. The plan was to formulate rules, which should apply henceforth in the whole United States. The result, however, was still more new playing rules and still more special hands. In place of the mysterious and exotic character of mahjong, once cherished, the element of sensational fairground attractions was added to the game. Moreover, the League changes its special hands each year and adds new rules, simply to increase the excitement.

The unmistakable advantage of the National Mah Jongg League is that Americans from all parts of their great and outstretched country could again play mahjong with each other without first talking for hours about the playing rules. Aboard a luxury cruise ship each year an international championship takes place with many enthusiastic participants from the whole United States of America. For a week the ship cruises the waters of the Eastern Caribbean, while on board the clattering of the mahjong tiles overwhelms the ears. The cost of the cruise starts at $999. The first prize for the winning player is a nice trophy and a check for $2000.

The National Mah Jongg League has thousands of enthusiastic members. They pay a yearly membership fee and receive in return a card with the playing rules of the current year. Besides that the league sells mahjong products, can replace lost tiles, and will arbitrate in mahjong quarrels.

As one enthusiastic member reports, "In the past the league consisted almost completely of older Jewish ladies, but that is changing fast. More and more youngsters become enthusiasts but women are still in the majority. My wife's grandmother plays every Wednesday with a group of women. We play it every Tuesday night after work. Between five and eight players, men and women, arrive at our home. If there are seven or eight of us then we have two tables. If there are six people or less we play in turn at one table. Until 11:00 we play as many rounds as possible. We have snacks and drinks. We talk a lot and enjoy each other's company. We play for money, but very little. We have agreed that one cannot lose more than $3 on a given evening. We play for fun, not for profit."

The newsletter has a question and answer section, as well as a place for members to sing their praises: "I've played mahjong for many, many years and I am really fond of this game and therefore I am grateful to our great league, because it is always ready with solutions for all our problems," wrote one member. Another member submitted this whimsical poem:

In my house lays a cloud of dust.
Oh, if you once saw that grubby mess.
But it doesn't bother me much.
Because I play Maj the whole day long!

The members talk mostly about *Maj* when they mean mahjong. The name Maj shows clearly that the game is completely Americanized. The majority of league members think that they are playing a centuries-old game. But in fact, Maj is a weak extract of the basic rules—many rules have been thrown away, and many new rules have been introduced.

The main differences are:

- Maj is played with 152 tiles;
- There are eights bonus tiles, called flowers;
- There are eight Joker tiles;
- The winning combinations are decided yearly by the league and distributed on a playing card; and
- The game doesn't recognize Chows but does recognize the sequence of five tiles known as the Quint.

Playing Material

If you want to play according to the rules of the National Mah Jongg League, you have to possess a mahjong set with 152 tiles: 136 regular tiles, 8 bonus tiles, and 8 Jokers. You will also need colored chips for the scores and mahjong racks with pins to stack your chips.

The set with which you can play the league rules is about twice as expensive as a common Chinese set.

Bonus Tiles

The four flowers and the four seasons

The mahjong cruises on the Caribbean Sea are very popular.

All the bonus tiles are equal and are all called flowers, regardless of their text, or number.

If you pick a bonus tile, you don't have to expose it, but you may use it in your hand. If the bonus tile does not work in your hand, then you can discard it.

Jokers

Jokers are an American invention and are not included in Chinese mahjong sets. Therefore the League sells stickers with which you can transform any tile into a Joker. Later mahjong sets were introduced to the market with eight Jokers in their assortment. The Jokers appear in many varieties. They often have a quasi-eastern picture and the inscription JOKER, so no mistakes can arise. If you have a set without Jokers, the League can deliver suitable Joker tiles for $3 to $4 apiece.

Several Joker tiles

With a Joker you can replace a lacking or impossible tile. Thanks to the Jokers the most impossible mahjongs can be obtained. Jokers replace every tile in a Pung and a Kong and can even produce a most remarkable sequence, the Quint—more to come on this in a moment.

If a Joker is exposed in a sequence at the table, any player may switch it with the tile it replaces, provided that it is his turn. A Joker that you pick up in this way can immediately be used in an exposed sequence or you can place it on your rack.

However, if you've exposed a sequence without Jokers, then you may not use a Joker to replace one of those tiles.

Jokers may not be used for a single or for a pair.

Jokers may not be used in the Charleston but may be discarded during the game. If you discard, then you announce "Same" or "Same tile," but not "Joker."

You can discard a Joker because:
• You're trying to obtain a hand in which no Jokers are allowed;

- You have a ready hand and need only to complete a pair or to obtain a single tile;
- You are after an extra double with a hand that does not allow Jokers; or
- You fear a winning hand from one of the other players.

A Joker is a safe tile to discard. No one can claim a discarded Joker.

Quint

A Quint is a sequence of five identical tiles. This king-size combination is necessary for certain mahjongs in the rules of the League. At least one Joker is necessary to create a Quint, because there are only four copies of every tile in a mahjong set. The league does not recognize a Chow.

The Joker helps you create a Pung, a Kong, and a Quint.

Dragons

The White Dragon can represent the number 0 if that is necessary for certain combinations. It is colorless and can be used with every suit—Characters, Bamboos, or Circles. Maj players usually call the White Dragon "soap."

Chips

Maj players count with chips. At the beginning of a game, every player receives twenty-four plastic coins at a value of 1000 points:

2 chips of	200	= 400 points
4 chips of	100	= 400 points
6 chips of	25	= 150 points
10 chips of	5	= 50 points

Seating Arrangements

The League does not have forced seating rules.

Building and Breaking the Wall

Since you play with 152 tiles, the walls are extra long—19 tiles each. East throws two dice and, starting with the East wall, counts from right to left. The wall is broken at that point. Starting with East, the players draw their tiles in turns.

Playing Card

Now it is time to examine the playing card of the League.

The playing card of the National Mah Jongg League lists all the allowed hands.

The League card displays all the hands with which you can go mahjong. The number is between fifty and sixty. Only the hands on the card are allowed. League members have quite a job at the beginning of a new "Maj year" to learn all the combinations by heart. Mostly they don't, and they play with the folded card sitting in front of them. The winning hands are subdivided into chapters like Anniversaries, Even Numbers, Any Like Numbers, Consecutive Runs, Quints, NEWS-Dragons, and Singles and Pairs.

Example 1:

There you are, sharing a table with three ladies who call themselves Betty, Betsy, and Ann. Outside the Caribbean floats along, but you don't notice it. The hall is chock-full of mahjong players, most of whom are women, which proves wrong the assertion that mahjong is not a ladies' game. For husbands who travel along there is a card tournament in an adjoining hall at the same time. However you came for the First Prize of the Maj tournament—$2,000—and therefore you have directed all your attention to the three-folded playing card.

"Consecutive Runs" says your card and beneath you read:

FF 1111 2222 DDDD .... X 25

The whole run is printed in one color. It means:

FF—any two flowers

1111 2222—two consecutive Kongs of one suit. For instance: a Kong of 6-Characters and a Kong of 7-Characters.

DDDD—four Dragons of the matching color. If your Kongs are of the Character suit then you need the Red Dragons.

X—exposed. Your Kongs can be exposed at the table.

25—This hand brings in 25 points.

This hand satisfies the playing card.

Because you did not use any Jokers, you get one double as bonus: 50 points.

For the same hand three Jokers have been used.

This hand with three Jokers is rewarded with 25 points.

Example 2:

Under the header "1998" of the playing card it reads:

FF 1998 1998 1998 .... C 50

The numbers have three different colors. You have to make this mahjong with any two flowers and the runs 1-9-9-8 in each of the three suits. The hand must be concealed, closed, and is rewarded with 50 points.

Example 3:
Beneath the header "Odd Numbers" is:
FFFF 2222 8888 10 .... X 25

Everything is printed in one color.

So for this hand you need: four of any flower, a Kong of 2-tiles, a Kong of 8-tiles of the same suit and a "pair," which is comprised of a 1-tile of the same suit and a White Dragon, which counts here as a 0 (zero).

The hand may be exposed and is rewarded with 25 points.

Charleston

Maj players also start their games with an obligatory Charleston. If all players are in favor of a second Charleston, it is played afterward. After one or two Charlestons you may change one last time with your opposite player, if you both agree to it. One, two, or three tiles may be exchanged. If you want to trade three tiles and he or she only one, than the lowest offer applies and so only one tile is switched.

Winning

A Pung, a Kong, a Quint, or any other sequence gives no points. The winner is the only one who scores. He receives points from the other players based on what the hand is worth. He may double his score if his winning hand contains no Jokers.

When he draws his winning tile from the wall, then his score doubles also. When he picks the winning tile from the table, then the player who discarded the winning tile pays double and the others do not pay anything.

The other players do not settle their scores. Only winning is rewarded with points.

Draw

Maj has no dead wall and no loose tiles. If you make a Kong or a Quint you don't have to draw a loose tile. Each winning hand contains only fourteen tiles, even when it contains Kongs and Quints. The game ends with a draw when the whole wall is exhausted and nobody has gone out. When it comes to a draw (a "wall game"), the East Wind passes to the next player, South.

Bettor

The League has invented the following variation to accommodate a five-player game: four persons start playing mahjong and the fifth player bets on who will win the hand. When the Charleston is completed and before the real game begins, he looks at everyone's hand and then places his bet. A small disc called a bettor was developed, which the League sells. The disc has four numbers: 1 for East, 2 for South, 3 for West, and 4 for North, and the fifth player uses this to indicate who he is betting on to win the game.

Three chimpanzees of a New York zoo also play mahjong, the newspapers report in January 1925. Unfortunately, the writer did not mention the rules with which they play and who plays the fourth Wind.

If the bettor believes that West will win, he turns the disc to 3. Of course, you can also take a piece of paper and write 3 on it.

If West indeed wins, the bettor receives from the three losers as many points as the winner. If West doesn't win, then the bettor pays the winner as many points as the losers pay him.

You can also bet on a draw. When it comes to a draw, then the bettor receives from each player the lowest score on the playing card: 25 points.

Service

The National Mah Jongg League does not organize competitions or tournaments. If you are a member you will receive your playing card and the newsletter, but you have to seek other players yourself. However, the League offers service and support. It answers all your questions about the game and arbitrates in disputes. You can buy all kinds of stuff: sets, extra tiles, a handbook, purses for chips, table covers, sweaters, and T-shirts. It supports charitable organizations and it sponsors the yearly mahjong cruise in the Caribbean.

Military Mahjong

The mahjong craze also made inroads in the U.S. Army, but here, discipline and a climate of control and orderliness prevented a proliferation of rules. In the 1920s, the rules were already fixed on Wright Patterson Air Force Base in Ohio. These rules still apply, with few changes, to almost all American military bases in the world.

The Officers Club of the Wright Patterson Air Force Base in Ohio

The most striking aspect of the Army's playing rules is the enormous amount of unique and often bizarre special hands, of which the American soldiers are so proud that they copyrighted them.

Mahjongers about Mahjong

Mahjong is often played on special occasions, such as birthdays, Thanksgiving, and Christmas. These holidays are considered family holidays—a time when family should get together and enjoy the company of one another. However, mahjong seems to take precedence and the meaning of the gathering is lost. Holidays are not what they used to be. The meaning of special holidays is lost in other priorities, such as Christmas shopping, or in this case mahjong.

—*Wai Ling Cheng, student, USA*

On Sundays the Chinese families who would come down to Chinatown to do their grocery shopping always ended up at our house and the mothers and fathers would play mahjong at our house until late at night. I'd say 10 or 12 families would come over to our house, so there were lots of kids. After supper, the living room and dining room were full of mahjong tables, and the kids stayed in our large kitchen. That was in the days of the radio.

—*Dorothy Moy, USA*

Father and mother invited the Sandersons, two neighbors who lived around the corner, to play mahjong at our home. Mr. and Mrs. Sanderson did not know the game so mother had to teach them the rules. We, the children, were never allowed to watch it. We were sent to Uncle Jack's. Mahjong was thought to be unseemly for children.

—*Charles Merz, USA*

What makes mahjong so special is the special atmosphere, which always accompanies it and which is difficult to define. What it is exactly I still do not know. The clamor of the tiles? The lamentations and the excitement of the players? The wall that each time has to be built again? Perhaps it was mainly the fascination for another culture, so different from ours—one not so transitory, so hurried, so commercial, or so soft from luxury. I mean who could imagine mahjong—the Winds, the Dragons? Even good ole Walt Disney could not invent such a thing.

—*Eric Kelman, USA*

My grandfather is the best mahjong player I ever saw. Often he breaks apart a nice hand to prevent discarding a tile with which he would lose the game. It is very hard to see when he has a nice hand, because he never sorts his tiles and nobody understands where his discarded tiles come from.

—Wei-Hwa Huang, USA

Our rules for playing mah jong have been passed through four generations of the Ming Family. Our rules are very simplified and contain a certain sense of fairness, while still allowing for vigorous competition. The Ming Family took the rules with them, when they emigrated from Canton, China, to America in 1876.

—Larry Ming, USA

JAPAN

Nowhere else in the world is mahjong played as much as it is in Japan. The game was introduced to Japan by the soldier Saburo Hirayama who, during his army years in China, came under the spell of the Game of the Hundred Wonders. To his sadness, once back in his home country he couldn't find anyone to play mahjong with. Therefore, in 1924, he started a mahjong school and a mahjong parlor, the Nan-nan Club in Tokyo, where Japanese intellectuals were quickly charmed by the game. Among the first addicts could be counted important writers, artists, and a celebrated actress, but soon thereafter the game became a craze all over Japan. Mahjong sets and instruction books sold like hotcakes. Anything with even the slightest connection to mahjong sold out in record time. From time to time the police had to arrest the most passionate gamblers of the mahjong game, but that only increased the popularity of the game even more. In 1924 the first nationwide tournament was held, but it could not contend with the different playing regulations used in all parts of Japan. That led to the foundation of the Japanese Mahjong League, which formulated uniform rules for the whole country and thus prevented the confusion that in the West caused many players to give up the game.

When war broke out with China in 1931, mahjong was forbidden. But the Japanese kept on playing. After the catastrophic Second World War, mahjong became even more popular than it was before. Mahjong parlors arose everywhere and became places where businessmen treated their clients and where youngsters sat around the mahjong tables until late at night, wrapped up in a thick mist of blue cigarette smoke. Students, especially, became addicted to the exotic game. They forgot their lessons and passed continuous days at the mahjong tables.

With the economic prosperity of the eighties and nineties of the last century, interest in mahjong decreased. Businessmen could now afford to take their guests to the golf course and the students preferred other night amusement than that "old people's sport." Ashamed by the game's stigma, the elderly stopped their game, which they had played for so long and with such a passion and pleasure. They stayed home with no other amusement than watching the television and no other excitement than switching from one channel to another.

Recently, however, youngsters have rediscovered the game through the Internet and software and have once again become addicted to the tempting game. Therefore mahjong is nowadays more popular than ever before. There is even a mahjong museum in Chiba with a sizeable collection that shows the origin and the history of the game. The number of mahjong parlors is unheard of: twenty-two thousand in all of Japan, five thousand in Tokyo, and twenty-five hundred in Osaka. The new generation of players prefers the fast, sensational "Riichi" variant.

The Mahjong Museum in Chiba shows the history and the variety of mahjong with its impressive collection.

Mahjongers about Mahjong

In Japan we play mahjong in a playing parlor, which is called "Janso." We pay a kind of entrance fee to play mahjong there. A Janso is not an elaborate place. At the entrance is a bar where we can buy food and drinks. The place is not big. There are ten mahjong tables. We mostly use the automatic mahjong table, which deals the tiles and builds the wall automatically. That is very handy.

Most people in Janso are fervent smokers, so it's always blue from smoke. We usually play from late at night until dawn. We think that mahjong is an exciting game and we often forget the time. Come and visit Janso—there you will always find friends to play a game of mahjong with.

—Takeaaki Nishioka, Akira Hirai, So-taro Kukita, students, Japan

Nowadays youngsters do not play mahjong. They think it is a dull game. They are richer than the generation of their parents and they have a different nightlife. That is probably quite healthier than sitting in a mahjong parlor until the early morning, where it is blue from cigarette smoke. Mahjong was the game of the meager years. It does not fit into the individualistic lifestyle of these years of abundance.

—*Masaki Okada, executive, Japan*

During my solo sailing trip around the world I was about to go crazy from terrible withdrawal symptoms. In Port Said in Egypt, my friends rescued me again. I had not played mahjong for one year. We played it in front of the pyramids. It was remarkably enjoyable. In the middle of the game, a security guard came over to disrupt us since he thought that we were selling something. By the way, I have since lost my mahjong skills. I have been away from the game too long to win.

—*Tatsuyo Watanabe, solo sailor, Japan*

Traditional Mahjong

Traditional Japanese mahjong is fast, because the scoring system is simplified. Only the winner gets points and the losers don't settle mutually. So only winning is rewarded and not elaborate tile combinations. Therefore, you have to play defense (trying to keep other players from gaining points) as well as offense (trying to win as quickly as possible). Japanese mahjong demands ingenuity and insight and diminishes the element of luck. Even a player with bad tiles has a chance to win. The gameplay is characterized by order and precision. Tradition and symbolism are important values.

Mahjong Set

A Japanese mahjong set looks somewhat different than a Western one. The tiles bear few Western numbers. There are no special tiles for the White Dragon. Completely blank tiles are used instead. Bonus tiles are absent, because the Japanese don't like to play with them. And one 5-Bamboo tile, one 5-Character tile, and one 5-Circles tile are painted with red paint. The tiles are called the "Red Fives" and sometimes used in the Riichi variant. A Red Five doubles your score, provided that it is agreed on beforehand.

Sticks

The Japanese play with three different sticks, which have values of respectively 500, 100, and 10 points. Every player gets:

2 sticks of 500 (with 6 red and 6 black dots)	= 1000 points
9 sticks of 100 (with 2 red dots)	= 900 points
10 sticks of 10 (with 8 red dots)	= 100 points
Total	= 2000 points

The sticks with the eight black dots, which are used in the West for 2 points, are not used.

Seating Arrangement

The official opening ceremony is even more complicated than the Old Chinese game. The four players are seated in an arbitrary order. One of them throws the dice, it does not matter whom, but it is polite to give that honor to the host. After that he counts counterclockwise, beginning with himself, the number shown on the dice. This indicates which player is temporary East.

Now the four Wind tiles—East, South, West, and North—are placed face-down, mixed, and placed in a row. An even-numbered tile and an odd-numbered tile are placed at the ends of the row, right-side up. The even-numbered tile is placed on one end of the row, and the odd-numbered tile is placed on the other.

The four concealed Wind tiles with an even tile on one side and an odd one on the other side

Now temporary East throws the dice and, beginning with himself, counts counterclockwise the number of thrown eyes, and indicates a player. If the throw is even, this player draws the Wind tile from the even end of the row; if the throw was odd, he picks the Wind tile from the odd end.

Now the other players draw the next Wind tiles from the same side of the row, and in this way establish their mutual seating arrangement at the table.

After this the player who drew the East tile lets the dice determine who may start the game. He counts up his throw counterclockwise, beginning with himself, and thus appoints the ultimate East. The player to the right of East becomes South, the next player West, and the following player North.

Fast Variant

The opening ceremony is so complicated that a very simple variant came into vogue: the oldest player at the table is automatically appointed as East. This is out of respect for the eldest player—the oldest person is also the wisest one, so the place of honor is for him. The other players remain seated and become South, West, and North.

Building the Wall

There are 136 tiles in the game. So the walls will be seventeen tiles long. The tiles are mixed by all four players or by East and West together. The Japanese prefer that you build the wall in the following way: with each hand, you pick up three stacks of two tiles and assemble them in a row. Again you pick up with both hands three stacks of two tiles and place them left and right of the row. Then you pick up three stacks of two with one hand and two stacks with the other, and attach them to both sides of the row. The four walls are pushed together until the corners touch each other. Since the Japanese don't use racks, you have to grasp your wall firmly at the two sides and push it carefully to the center of the table.

Dealing the Tiles

The tiles are picked up in groups of four until everyone has twelve tiles. After that East draws his thirteenth and fourteenth tile, the thirteenth draw being the first tile of the wall and the fourteenth draw being the fourth tile, such that the dealer skips across the top of the live wall to take these two last tiles. The Japanese call this *chon-chon*, which is a sound-word representing the rhythm of the dealer's last two draws. The other players draw their thirteenth tile in turn. Japanese players place their tiles upright in a row before them.

Dead Wall

The fourteen tiles of the dead wall are clearly separated. No loose tiles are placed on the dead wall. The dead wall is constantly replenished.

Discarding

Tiles are not discarded at random. Every player puts them neatly in rows in front of herself, from left to right, so it is easy to see which tiles are discarded and in which order. This is of importance for the rule of Dangerous Discards (more on this to come).

When you make a Chow, a Pung, or a Kong you place the claimed tile cross-wise to the others. If the tile comes from the player at your left, then you put the tile at the left side; if it came from the player to your right, you place the tile at the right; and if it came from the player in front of you then you put the tile in the middle of your Chow or Pung. This allows everyone to know how your combinations were completed.

You got the Pung of East Winds from the player in front of you, the Kong of 3-Bamboos from the player to your right, and the Chow of Circles from the player left of you.

Speeding Up

To speed up the game the Japanese like to Chow, Pung, or Kong in the following way: they call Chow, Pung, or Kong, discard a tile so the turn goes immediately to the next player, expose two or three tiles, and add the discarded tile to it.

Going Out

No Doubles are needed to go out. Every completed hand is allowed. Doubles are called "Fan" and pronounced as "han" in Japanese. The Chinese use the same word for a Double but pronounce it as "fa-an."

Sacred Discard

The only restricting rule is the rule of the Sacred Discard, which is as follows: If any of the tiles needed to complete your hand are in your discard pile, you may not go mahjong using an opponent's discard. This applies whether or not the opponent's discard is one of the tiles in your discard pile. For example, if you are waiting for a 2-, 5-, or 8-Bamboo, and early in the game you accidentally discarded a 2-Bamboo, and your opponent discards an 8-Bamboo, you may not declare mahjong and complete your hand. The same applies when an opponent discards a 2- or 8-Bamboo: once you have discarded one of the tiles that you yourself need to complete your hand, all discards are off-limits for declaring mahjong, and you can only complete your hand by drawing the winning tile yourself.

This hand waits for a 6-Bamboo or a 9-Bamboo.

Example: You have a Waiting Hand with a waiting Chow of 7-Bamboo and 8-Bamboo. Earlier during the game you discarded 9-Bamboo. One of the other players also now discards a 9-Bamboo. Regrettably, since you already discarded that tile, you are forbidden to claim any discards because a needed tile is in your discard pile. The only possibility to obtain mahjong is drawing 9-Bamboo or 6-Bamboo from the wall.

Points

Winning is rewarded with 20 points. If you draw the winning tile from the wall, you get 2 extra points. The Only Possible Tile also earns 2 points. Kong, Pungs, and Chows are rewarded the same as in basic mahjong.

You get Fan (Doubles) for the following combinations:

Pung/Kongs of Dragons	1 Fan
Pung/Kongs of own Winds	1 Fan
Pung/Kongs of prevailing Winds	1 Fan
All Pungs	1 Fan
Concealed tiles 1 through 9 of one suit	2 Fan
Exposed tiles 1 through 9 of one suit	1 Fan
Three concealed Pungs	1 Fan

Fan for Special Hands

Winning without points	1 Fan + 10 points

This hand (known as "Pinghu" in Japanese):
- Should be concealed, except for the winning tile;
- May not have points;
- Contains only Chows and a pair of Simple tiles;
- The winning tile is not drawn from the wall; and
- The winning tile is not the only possible tile.

All Simples	1 Fan
All Honors and Terminals	1 Fan
All concealed Honors and Terminals	1 Fan
Cleared hand	1 Fan
Pure hand	3 Fan + 10 points
Little Three Dragons	1 Fan
Concealed hand	1 Fan
Bottom of the Sea	1 Fan
Bottom of the River	1 Fan
Winning with loose tile	1 Fan
Robbing a Kong	1 Fan

Special Hands

The following special hands are permitted:

Three Dragons	limit
Little Four Winds	limit
Four Winds	limit
All Honors	limit
All Terminals	limit
Four concealed Pungs	limit
Thirteen Orphans	limit
Nine Gates	limit
Heaven's Blessing	limit
Earth's Blessing	limit

Note: If you're winning with the first tile you draw from the wall, you may not have a Kong, a Pung, or a Chow. Be aware that this rule differs from the usual definition.

Limit

The limit is 500 points. When you are East you earn double: 3 x 1000 = 3000 points. If you are another Wind, then you earn 2 x 500 + 1 x 1000 = 2000 points.

Variant: The limit is often raised to 1500 points.

Steady Wind

When East wins she keeps the deal and so she gets an extra turn. She puts a stick of 10 points in front of her to mark that she has an extra deal.

Besides her own score, the winner of this extra deal gets 100 points from every loser or 300 points from the player who discarded the winning tile.

If East wins again she gets her score in addition to these 300 points. They are not doubled.

Now East puts a second stick of 10 points on the table to mark her second extra deal. The winner now gets 200 extra points from every loser or 600 points from the player who discarded the winning tile.

If there is a third extra deal the winner gets 900 extra points, and so on.

When East wins eight extra hands she receives the limit from the losers, but now the deal goes to the next player.

Note: This rule works when a limit of 1500 points is agreed upon.

Draw

It is only a draw if the live wall is exhausted and no one has declared mahjong. This is the official rule, but for many Japanese there are four more possibilities for a draw:

- If at the beginning of the game nine of your thirteen tiles are different major tiles. You have to announce this immediately.
- If four Kongs in total are claimed in a single game. The player who forms the fourth Kong is not permitted to pick up an extra tile. Robbing a Kong is allowed.
- If in the first turn the same tile is discarded four times in succession.
- If three players claim the same discarded tile.

After a draw the deal passes from East to the next player.

Only Winning Counts

In Japanese mahjong only the winner scores. The Japanese believe that this rule gives the game more excitement. It forces the players to compete more with each other.

There is always one winner but there could be one or three losers. There is one loser when mahjong is declared with his discarded tile. The discarding player has to pay the winner also on behalf of the two other players; this means four times the score of the winner. If East is the winner, then the guilty player has to pay six times the score of the winner.

There are three losers when a player obtains mahjong by drawing the winning tile from the wall. Then all three losers pay him his score and East has to double his payment. If East is the winner then the other players pay the double score.

As a result, the players are forced to be attentive to the intentions of the other players, because the player who discards the winning tile loses painfully. For the winner it makes no difference where his winning tile comes from, the wall or the table. In both cases he gets paid his score four or six times.

Counting Made Easier

To facilitate the counting the winner places:

* The winning tile upright for Only Possible Tile;

With an upright-placed tile, the winner claims 2 points for Only Possible Tile.

* The winning tile flat down on top of the winning combination, indicating Self-Drawn;

A flat tile makes it clear that the winning tile is drawn from the wall.

- The winning tile upright on top of the winning combination for both Only Possible Tile and Self-Drawn;

This indicates that the winning tile is the Only Possible Tile and drawn from the wall.

- A tile flat on top of a combination indicating a concealed Pung;
- The other series are shown in the normal way.

Settling the Score

The scores are first doubled and then rounded off to the nearest tenfold—for example, 24 becomes 20, 26 becomes 30.

Example: You win with a tile from the wall and have 32 points and 3 Fan, then your score will be 32 x 2 x 2 x 2 = 256. Rounded off this is 260. You receive 260 points from two players each and from East, 2 x 260 = 520 (and not 2 x 256 = 512, rounded off 510). The Japanese use handy tables.

Table for Winning with Discarded Tile

If East draws the winning tile from the table, then the losers pay him according to the first red column. If one of the other players wins, then the losers pay him according to the second column:

	0 Fan	1 Fan	2 Fan	3 Fan	4 Fan	5 Fan
20	120 80	240 160	480 320	960 640	1920 1280	3000 2000
22	120 80	240 160	540 360	1080 720	2100 1400	3000 2000
24	120 80	300 200	600 400	1140 760	2280 1520	3000 2000
26	180 120	300 200	600 400	1260 840	2520 1680	3000 2000
28	180 120	360 240	660 440	1320 880	2700 1800	3000 2000
30	180 120	360 240	720 480	1440 960	2880 1920	3000 2000
32	180 120	360 240	780 520	1560 1040	3000 2000	3000 2000

34	180 120	420 280	840 560	1620 1080	3000 2000	3000 2000
36	240 160	420 280	840 560	1740 1160	3000 2000	3000 2000
38	240 160	480 320	900 600	1800 1200	3000 2000	3000 2000
40	240 160	480 320	960 640	1920 1280	3000 2000	3000 2000
42	240 160	480 320	1020 680	2040 1260	3,000 2000	3000 2000
44	240 160	540 360	1080 720	2100 1400	3000 2000	3000 2000
46	300 200	540 360	1080 720	2200 1480	3000 2000	3000 2000
48	300 200	600 400	1140 760	2280 1520	3000 2000	3000 2000
50	300 200	600 400	1200 1600	2400 1600	3000 2000	3000 2000

Table for Winning with Self-Drawn

If East draws his winning tile from the wall, then all players pay him according to the red columns; if he draws the winning tile from the wall then the winner is paid according to the second column:

	0 Fan	1 Fan	2 Fan	3 Fan	4 Fan	5 Fan
20	40 20	80 40	160 80	320 160	640 320	1000 500
22	40 20	80 40	180 90	360 180	700 350	1000 500
24	40 20	100 50	200 100	380 190	760 380	1000 500
26	60 30	100 50	200 100	420 210	840 420	1000 500
28	60 30	120 60	220 110	440 220	900 450	1000 500
30	60 30	120 60	240 120	480 240	960 480	1000 500
32	60 30	120 60	260 130	520 260	1000 500	1000 500
34	60 30	140 70	280 140	540 270	1000 500	1000 500
36	80 40	140 70	280 140	580 290	1000 500	1000 500
38	80 40	160 80	300 150	600 300	1000 500	1000 500
40	80 40	160 80	320 160	640 320	1000 500	1000 500
42	80 40	160 80	340 170	680 340	1000 500	1000 500
44	80 40	180 90	360 180	700 350	1000 500	1000 500
46	100 50	180 90	360 180	740 370	1000 500	1000 500
48	100 50	200 100	380 190	760 380	1000 500	1000 500
50	100 50	200 100	400 200	800 400	1000 500	1000 500

Riichi

Riichi is extremely popular among Japanese youngsters, but even outside Japan the game is gaining fast in popularity. Europe has a growing number of devoted Riichi players and tournaments are taking place on a regular basis.

Riichi is fast and exciting with a lot of possible points. The counting system is simple, but there are so many combinations possible that Riichi has made mahjong difficult again. The number of Fan (Doubles) can increase considerably. Therefore playing offensively is the best tactic; you have to go out as soon as possible. In the 1950s Riichi was played by professional gamblers and crooks who, crazily enough, popularized the game and left their mark on the way it is played—because nowadays Riichi players still disdain Pungs and Chows, which were especially hated by the crooks, and love the gambling element, which is abundantly present in a lot of house rules.

Riichi means "ready" and is called by the player who has a waiting hand and needs only one tile to go out. It doesn't matter if he needs a special tile or that he has several possibilities. He calls "Riichi" (pronounced "ree-chy") and puts a chip of 1,000 points in front of him.

If he goes out, he gets an extra bonus in the form of a Yaku (more on this to come). And he gets his 1,000 points back. There are some exceptions, but these will be discussed later.

Chips

That Riichi mahjong is all about a lot of points becomes immediately clear when distributing the chips. Every player gets:

1 chip of 10,000	= 10,000	points
2 chips of 5000	= 10,000	points
9 chips of 1000	= 9000	points
10 chips of 100	= 1000	points

This is in total 30,000 points of chips. So you can win or lose a lot. Elongated "bones" or the brightly colored plastic coins, which you see often in gambling games, are used as chips.

To speed up the game, score cards are used to track the gains and losses. Japanese mahjong parlors have mahjong tables that automatically count the score. Usually Riichi is played for money—from 30 to 100 yen per 1,000 points. Gambling is forbidden in Japan, but since the gambling amounts in Riichi are so small, no one interferes.

氏名 回数	記録帳 Kees +	Kees −	Frans +	Frans −	Mathij +	Mathij −	Ruud +	Ruud −	+	−
1		1800	2000	6300	18000			9600			
2		4200		9400	9600			1000			
3	2000	2000			1000			8000			
4		6300			4200			6300			
5		8400			2000			1400			
6					18900						
小計					26200						
差引				−13700							
備考	− 28900		+ 73900				− 53300				

A preprinted score card from Japan

Allocation of Seats

The allocation of seats around the table happens quickly. The four Wind tiles, an odd tile, and an even one are mixed and placed in a row. The oldest player (or the host) throws two dice. The six tiles are turned faceup and the odd and the even tiles are moved to the closest side.

The six tiles are turned.

3-Circles and 8-Bamboo are moved to the left and right side.

If the oldest player throws an odd number, then he gets the Wind that is on the odd side temporarily—in this case, West. The other players are allocated the other temporary Winds: the player who sits right of the oldest (counterclockwise) gets the second Wind (East); the player who sits right of him gets the third Wind (South); and the fourth player gets the remaining Wind (North).

If the oldest player throws an even number, then he becomes North and the other players respectively become South, East, and West.

Now temporary East decides who will become East by throwing the dice. If he throws six, for instance, then he counts counterclockwise, starting with himself, and temporary South becomes East. With the same dice roll final East counts six tiles from the right side of his wall to open it.

Dora

Bonus tiles are not used, so the walls are seventeen tiles long. East throws two dice to decide which wall will be opened. The player of this wall counts from the right the thrown number of eyes and opens the wall. (The dice are thrown only one time.) He turns also the third tile at the end of the dead wall, so that its picture becomes visible. This tile is called the Dora Indicator. The tile that comes next in order from the Dora Indicator becomes the Dora for that hand. Each Dora used in a completed hand scores an extra Fan.

The third to the last tile of the dead wall is turned. 2-Character is the turning tile, so 3-Character is the Dora and is worth an extra Double.

If the Dora Indicator is 1, the Dora is 2 of the same suit. If the Dora Indicator is 9, the Dora is the 1 of the same suit. The order of the Winds and Dragons is used to determine which tile becomes the Dora when a Wind or a Dragon becomes the Dora Indicator. The order for the Winds is E-S-W-N, so that when E is the Dora Indicator, S is the Dora; when N is the Dora Indicator, E is the Dora. The order is White-Green-Red for the Dragons, such that when the Dora Indicator is White Dragon, the Dora is Green Dragon; when it is Red, the Dora is White Dragon.

Note: The sequence of the Dragons is alphabetical: Green, Red, White. You can use this as a memory aid.

Doras are so popular with the Japanese, that often more Dora rules are added to the game. So always confirm which extra Dora rules will be considered valid. The most used variants are:

- If you have announced Riichi and you go out, then the tile beneath the original turning tile will also become a turning tile. That is the Ura Dora.
- If you make a Kong, an extra Dora is appointed. The tile to the right of the last Dora Indicator (counterclockwise) is turned faceup and shows an additional Dora Indicator. This happens only after you discard your tile, unless you picked the fourth tile from the wall yourself. This procedure repeats after

every Kong, but not more than four times because by then the four Kong tiles are gone and the game has come to a draw.

After a Kong is made, two tiles lay open in the dead wall, so there are two Doras: 3-Character and 4-Bamboo.

Note: It is not wise to declare a Kong if a player has announced Riichi. The extra Dora gives this player an extra opportunity to a Double.

Red Five

An exceptional Dora rule is the Red Five. One 5-Bamboo, one 5-Character, and one 5-Circles, of a Japanese mahjong set are painted red. These tiles produce an extra Fan just as Doras.

Note: You can easily add some red fives to your game, even if you don't have a Japanese set. Rub the three tiles well with red paint or nail polish. If you want to play another type of mahjong afterward, just ignore the color of the red fives.

Bonus

At the beginning of the game each player donates 5,000 points to the pool. The winner of the game gets these 20,000 points on top of the points he earned.

Optional: You can also agree on the following extra bonuses: the player who loses (who becomes fourth) pays a bonus of 3,000 points to the winner and the player in third place pays a bonus of 1,500 points to the second place player.

Course of the Game

The course of the game is the same as in traditional Japanese mahjong.

Yaku

To go out you must have at least one Yaku. Yaku means "rule" and is the rule that determines under which circumstance you are allowed to go out. Yakus determine whether you can make a mahjong.

A game of 3 Yaku yields 3 Fan. But a Fan is not equal to a Yaku. Doras, for example, yield Fan, but no Yaku. You count your score with Fan. You can have a hand that yields 4 Fan but no single Yaku.

This hand scores 4 Fan if the Doras are 5-Circle and 8-Character, but it doesn't give a Yaku.

Optional: You can also agree that you must have 2, 3, or 4 Yaku to make mahjong.

Announcing Riichi

You can announce Riichi if you have a Waiting Hand. That produces an extra Yaku and gives you the opportunity to go out with a hand that otherwise would not score a Yaku. You say "Riichi," put a chip of 1,000 points in front of you, and close your hand. The first tile that you discard has to be laid down crosswise against the other tiles so that the other players can see easily which tiles you discarded since your Riichi announcement. You put the next tiles again in the normal way in front of you.

These are some conditions under which you may call Riichi:
- You must have a Waiting Hand. It doesn't matter if you need one particular tile or if there are several possibilities.
- The Waiting Hand must be fully concealed.
- You may not make changes after the announcement. You only may draw tiles from the wall and discard them, until you obtain mahjong.

Optional: Some players allow you to promote a concealed Pung to a concealed Kong with a tile from the wall and do not consider this an opening of your hand. Not everybody agrees with this exception.

Optional: You have to accept the first winning tile, even when it's not the best tile. Waiting for a better tile is forbidden. If you get caught doing this then you have to return this tile and, as a punishment, you must play with a dead hand. You cannot claim a tile from the table; only drawing from the wall is allowed.

Winning after Riichi

If you win then your score will be doubled and you get your chip of 1,000 points back. All chips go to the winner if other players announced Riichi and did not win. If you lose then you have lost your 1,000 points.

You are not obliged to call Riichi if you have a Waiting Hand.

You should only declare a Riichi if you are fairly certain that you will still be able to obtain a winning tile despite the announcement of your readiness. If you have a hand with at least one Yaku, then you don't have to announce Riichi to get a Yaku. It can even be foolish to do so since the other players will pay extra attention to your hand.

Hot Tile

Winning becomes more difficult by two rules of the Hot Tile, or "Fu ri ten," as the Japanese say:

- You are not allowed to go out with a tile you already discarded, unless you draw that tile from the wall and thus make a Tsumo.
- You are not allowed to go out with a Chow, if one of the tiles in the Chow was previously discarded by you. This restriction is called the 1-4-7-rule.

Example: You discard 4-Bamboo. Then you cannot go out anymore with 4-Bamboo. And you may not go out by finishing a potential Chow of 2-Bamboo and 3-Bamboo with a 1-Bamboo, because a 4-Bamboo also goes with 2-Bamboo and 3-Bamboo.

You also may not complete 5-Bamboo and 6-Bamboo with a 7-Bamboo, because 4-Bamboo also goes with a 5-Bamboo and 6-Bamboo.

Yet you are allowed to have a 5-Bamboo and a 7-Bamboo in your hand and to wait on a 6-Bamboo.

A tile from the wall is never hot and may always be used to go out, even if you discarded it before.

Missed Tile

Optional: If desired, the following rule of the Missed Tile can be observed: You may not claim the winning tile if that tile was discarded in the previous round. This rule gives the other players a better chance to discard a tile safely. This rule is not used often.

Penalties

You have to donate 1,000 points to the pool if you falsely call a Chow, Pung, or Kong. The pool goes to the winner.

If you are East and you falsely announce Riichi or mahjong, then you will be punished with 12,000 points (4,000 points to every player) or 8,000 points if you are another Wind (4,000 points to East and 2,000 points to the other players). The Wind advances to the next player and a new game starts.

If you forget to claim a tile and the same tile is discarded once more on the table, then you are not allowed to claim the tile in the same round.

Going out	20 points
Winning after a Riichi announcement	10 points
Winning tile from the wall	2 points
Winning with Only Possible Tile	2 points
Seven pairs	25 points

Kong, Pungs, and Chows score the same points as elsewhere.

Ron or Tsumo

There two ways to go out. In Riichi mahjong, it is called *ron* if you draw the winning tile from the table. It is called *tsumo* if you draw the winning tile from the wall. The difference is important for the losers. Experienced Riichi players don't call mahjong, but Ron or Tsumo.

With a Ron the player who discarded the winning tile pays for all players—that means four times the score of the winner (East pays double). If East is the winner then the discarder pays six times the score.

With a Tsumo all players pay one time the score, except East who has to pay double. If East wins all players pay him double.

For the winner there is no difference between Ron or Tsumo: he always receives four or six times his score.

Draw

The game comes to a draw:
• If the live wall is exhausted completely and only the fourteen tiles of the dead wall are left;

- If in the first turn all players discard the same Wind tile;
- If a fifth Kong is claimed; or
- If all players announced Riichi.

Variations:
- The game comes to a draw if a player has in his first turn nine different terminals and not a single Chow, Pung, or Kong. This player is allowed to go for mahjong and to try to turn his hand into the Thirteen Orphans, for instance;
- If three players claim the same discarded tile to go out; or
- If a player has no more chips.

When it comes to a draw you will receive 3,000 points from the other players if you have a Waiting Hand (you do not have to announce it). If two players have a Waiting Hand, each receives 1,500 points from the two other players. If three players are waiting then the fourth player has to pay 1,000 points to each.

Waiting Player	Receives	Others pay
1	3000	3 x 1000
2	1500	2 x 1500
3	1000	1 x 3000

No other points are settled when it is a draw. The chips that were put on the table by the Riichi announcements stay there and will be collected by the winner of the next game.

Extra Points

After East goes out, or when it comes to a draw, extra points can be earned.

After a draw, 300 points go into a fictitious pool for the winner of the next game. The person who pays these points is determined by the next game. The player who discards the winning tile has to pay the 300 points of the fictitious pool to the winner. If the winning tile is drawn from the wall, then the points of the pool are paid by the three losers—so 100 points each.

If it becomes a draw again, then the stake in the pool is raised by 300 points. After reaching a draw two times, the pool counts 600 points; after three times 900 points; after four times 1,200 points, and so on.

The same rule applies when East goes mahjong: 300 points are put in the pool for the winner of the next game. If East wins again then he gets paid the content of the pool and the stake into the pool is raised by 300 points. For instance, if East wins five times in a row he will receive 1,500 points from the pool after his fifth victory.

When East wins eight times in a row he is rewarded with a limit and the Wind changes.

Wind Changes

After every game the Wind changes, whether it ends in mahjong or in a draw. East becomes North and South becomes East. Only when East obtains mahjong, or has a waiting hand in the case of a draw, does the Wind not change.

End of the Game

A complete Riichi game consists of two rounds: the round of the East Wind and the round of the South Wind. Then the game is over.

Optional: The game is also over when East is the Wind eight consecutive times.

Optional: The game is over if a player has no more chips. When this rule applies you cannot lose more than 30,000 points in one Riichi game.

Penalty for Not Scoring

Optional: If you did not get a single mahjong during the two rounds of a complete Riichi game, you will get a severe penalty of 8,000 points at the end of the game. If you are East when the game ends your penalty will amount to 12,000 points.

Yaku

In Riichi, going mahjong is related mostly to the number of Fan you can score. There are plenty of opportunities to earn Fan. The winning tile can be claimed from the table, except in some special cases.

To easily recognize Yaku and Fan, the hands are sorted according to their patterns:

Yaku for Riichi and Doras

		Concealed	Exposed
Riichi announced		1	
Double Riichi	Daburi Riichi	2	

This applies if you announce Riichi in your first turn. No Kong, Pungs, or Chows may be claimed.

Instant Riichi	Ippatsu	2	

This applies if you go out in the turn after your Riichi announcement, without someone else getting a Kong, Pung, or Chow. The turn ends when you discard a tile again.

Dora		1	

This applies to every Dora in your hand.

Yaku for Special Hands

Winning with no points	Pinfu	1	

This is a completely concealed hand, except for the winning tile, and it may not score points. It consists only of Chows and a pair of Simple tiles. The winning tile cannot be the Only Possible Tile.

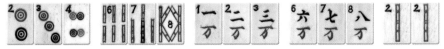

This hand is winning with no points if the winning tile is not: 3-Circles, 7-Bamboo, 2-Character, 7-Character, or 2-Bamboo, since these tiles will give points for Only Possible Tile.

Simple hand	Tanyao chuu	1	1

Only Simple tiles.

Fully concealed hand	Tsumo	1	

All tiles concealed, with the winning tile drawn from the wall.

Moon from the Bottom of the Sea	Haitei	1	1

Winning with last tile from the wall before a draw.

Fish from the Bottom of the River	Haitei	1	1

Winning with the last discarded tile before a draw.

Winning with a loose tile	Richan kaihou	1	1
Robbing a Kong	Kan tsu	1	1
Nine Gates	Chuuren pooto	13 or more	
Only Pungs	Suu ankou	13 or more	
Heaven's Blessing	Tenho	13 or more	
Earth's Blessing	Chiho	13 or more	

Winning with the first tile you draw from the wall; no Kongs, Pungs, or Chows may be claimed by others.

Note: This rule differs from the usual description.

Nobleman	Nagashi mangaan	13 or more	13 or more

Winning after you discarded only major tiles that were claimed by nobody and the play ends in a draw.

Yaku for Colors

Cleared-hand	Honitsu	3	2
Pure hand	Chinitsu	6	5
Imperial jade	Ryuu iisou	13 or more	13 or more

Yaku for Honors

Pung of Dragons	Fanpai	1	1
Pung of own Winds	Fanpai	1	1
Pung of prevailing Winds	Fanpai	1	1
Little Three Dragons	Shou gan gen	2	2
Big Three Dragons	Dai sangen	13 or more	13 or more
Little Four Winds	Shoo suushii	13 or more	13 or more
Big Four Winds	Dai suushii	13 or more	13 or more
Only Honors	Tsuu iisou	13 or more	13 or more

Yaku for Pungs and Kong

Only Pungs	Toi-toi	2	2
Three concealed Pungs	San ankou	2	2
Three Kongs	San kan tsu	2	2
Four concealed ascending Pungs of one suit	Suu renkou	13 or more	
Four Kongs	Suu kan tsu	13 or more	13 or more

Yaku for Similarity

Two equal Chows	Lipeikou	1	

Of one suit, only concealed.

Three equal Chows	Lisou sanjun	2	2
Mixed triple Chow	San shoku doujun	2	1

Three Chows of three suits with the same numbers.

Double two equal Chows	Ryan peikou	3	3
Four equal Chows	Yonjun	5	5
Triple Pung	San shoku dokou	3	3

Three Pungs of three suits with the same numbers.

Yaku for Successions

Pure straight	Itsu	2	1

Three ascending Chows in one suit.

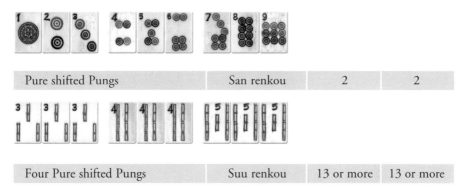

Pure shifted Pungs	San renkou	2	2

Four Pure shifted Pungs	Suu renkou	13 or more	13 or more

The four Pungs have to be of one suit.

Yaku for Honors and Terminals

Only Honors and Terminals	Honroutou	2	2
Concealed Honors and Terminals	Chanta	2	1

Honor and Terminal tiles in every combination, also in a pair.

Concealed Terminals	Junchan talyao	3	2

Terminals in every combination, also in a pair.

Only Terminals	Chinrouto	13 or more	13 or more

Yaku for Singles and Twins

Thirteen Orphans	Koku shimusou	13 or more	
Seven pairs	Chii toitsu	2	

Seven arbitrary pairs of all kind of tiles; four same tiles are not allowed.

Climbing pairs	Dai sharin	13 or more

Seven ascending pairs of Simple tiles and one suit.

Counting

Only the score of the winner is counted. The counting consists of three parts:

- The counting of the points;
- The counting of the fan; and
- The multiplying of points and fan.

Counting the Points

To simplify the counting the points are rounded up immediately to the nearest ten; thus 22 points, 24, 26, and 28 are all rounded up to 30 points.

Counting the Fan

To go out with one Yaku is obligatory. For a mahjong you automatically get two Fan extra. If you have more than four Fan then you don't have to count additional points since the counting is now solely in limits. Some examples of this will follow.

Multiplying

When multiplying the scored points with the Fan it is important to consider whether the mahjong was obtained with a tile from the wall (Tsumo) or with a tile from the table (Ron).

With Tsumo there are three losers who each pay the total score. The winner receives four times his score two times from East and one time from the two other players. If East is the winner then he gets two times his score from each player, six times in total.

With Ron there is one loser—the player who discarded the winning tile. He pays for everyone. When East is the loser he pays six times the score. If another player loses, that player pays four times the score.

When paying the amount, it is rounded up to the nearest hundred.

Example: You go out with a tile discarded by West, and so make Ron. Your score is 32 points. Rounded up, that is 40 points. You are entitled to two Fan and may add two extra doubles for going out—so four times doubling. That results in 640 points. West has to pay on behalf all players, four times in total (East 2 x, South 1 x, and West 1 x). Four times 640 points = 2,560, rounded up 2,600 points.

East	South	West	North
0	0	-2600	2600

Example: You draw your winning tile from the wall and so make Tsumo. You are North and your score is 34 points. Rounded up, that is 40 points. You are entitled to two Fan. So you may double four times. That result is 640 points. East pays you 2 x 640 = 1,280 = rounded up 1,300 points: South and West each pay you 640 points = rounded up 700 points. So you collect 1,300 + 700 + 700 = 2,700 points.

East	South	West	North
-1300	-700	-700	2700

Example: You are East and win for the third consecutive time, this time with Tsumo. You are entitled to three Fan and your score is 42 points. Rounded up that is 50 points. You may double 3 + 2 = 5 times. That results in 1,600 points. Because you are East everybody has to pay double: 3,200 points. Because you won three times in a row as East, you receive also the 900 points from the pool. South, West, and North each pay you 3,200 + 300 = 3,500 points, so you would collect 10,500 points total—if there was no limit!

With Tsumo there is a limit of 2,000 points and for East 4,000 points; with Ron the limit is 8,000 points and for East 12,000 points.

East	South	West	North
12,000	-4000	-4000	-4000

Because Riichi is played fast players do not want to waste their time with complicated calculations.

They prefer the use of handy tables in which everything is already calculated, including the two bonus doubles that are automatically scored by any winning hand.

Ron for East and Other Winds

The first column applies for East—if she makes Ron, she receives from the loser 1 x the red amount; the second column applies to the other players—if one of them makes Ron, he receives from the losers 1 x the black amount.

Score	1 fan	2 fan	3 fan	4 fan
20	1000 700	2000 1300	1300 700	2600 1300
25	-	2400 1600	1600 800	3200 1600
30	1500 1000	2900 2000	2000 1000	3900 2000
40	2000 1300	3900 2600	2600 1300	4000 2000
50	2400 1600	4800 3200	3200 1600	4000 2000
60	2900 2000	5800 3900	3900 2000	4000 2000
70	3400 2300	6800 4500	4000 2000	4000 2000

Tsumo for East and Other Winds

The first column applies for East—if he makes Tsumo he receives the red amount from the three losers. The second column applies to the other players: if one of them makes Tsumo he or she receives the black amount from two losers and the red amount from East.

Score	1 fan	2 fan	3 fan	4 fan
20	400 200	700 400	1300 700	2600 1300
25	-		1600 800	3200 1600
30	500 300	1000 500	2000 1000	3900 2000
40	700 400	1300 700	2600 1300	4000 2000
50	800 400	1600 800	3200 1600	4000 2000
60	1000 500	2000 1000	3900 2000	4000 2000
70	1200 600	2300 1200	4000 2000	4000 2000

Limit

For Tsumo a limit applies of 2,000 points and for East 4,000 points; for Ron the limit is 8,000 points and for East 12,000 points.

When you have more than four Fan you can stop counting your points since thereafter counting is solely done with limits. This will also help you keep track of your limits.

Table for Limits

Fan	Ron		Tsumo	
	East	Other	East	Other
5	12,000	8000	4000	2000
6-7	18,000	12,000	6000	3000
8-9-10	24,000	16,000	8000	4000
11-12	36,000	24,000	12,000	6000
13 or more	48,000	32,000	16,000	8000

Of course you can agree on other amounts for a limit. Then you have to obey the following doubling of limits:

5 fan	Limit
6-7 fan	One and half limit
8-9-10	Double limit
11-12 fan	Triple limit
more than 13 fan	Four double limit (= maximum)

Some Common Terms

Riichi — Announcement of a Waiting Hand. After this the hand may not be changed anymore.

Yaku — A rule which a combination has to obey

Fan — The bonus for a Yaku

Dora — Each Dora (special tile) used in your hand scores a bonus double.

Ippatsu — Winning in the first turn after Riichi is announced, without the other players claiming a discarded tile

Ron — Winning with a discarded tile

Tsumo — Winning with a tile drawn from the wall

Automatic Mahjong Tables

The Japanese produce automatic mahjong tables that mix the tiles and build the four walls. These automatic tables are now so common and prevalent that you can't think of Japanese mahjong parlors without them. And, since the new generation of mahjong players has learned the game using them, many youngsters don't know anymore how to mix the tiles and build a wall with their own hands.

In the middle of an automatic table four flaps are placed around the automatic dice. When you push one of the buttons the flaps open and you can push the tiles off the table into the opened hole. When you push the button one more time the flaps will close and four walls of 2 x 17 (or 18) tiles are pushed to the outside of the table. Pushing another button causes the dice to roll; it is only at this point that the players themselves have to act by opening the wall and collecting their tiles. From the inside of the table a rumbling and clattering mounts as the machine starts to mix the disposed tiles and build the four walls so they are ready for use when the button is pushed once again.

The automatic mahjong tables work with two mahjong sets of 136 tiles each (the bonus tiles aren't used). The sets only differ in the color of the backs of the tiles. Small magnets are placed inside the tiles to enable the machine to turn the pictures upside down and to build a tidy wall.

The prices of these tables vary from 40,000 to 700,000 yen, that is, from $400 to $7,000. For a mere $20,000 you can own a deluxe automatic table, which will do all the calculating for you as well. When you push a winning hand to the right side of this table it calculates the score for you. Moreover, it automatically counts (weighs, actually) the chips that you put in the drawers under the table and in this way keeps track of the scores of all players.

CHINA TODAY

INCLUDING THE CHINESE OFFICIAL INTERNATIONAL RULES, AND OTHER ASIAN VARIANTS

In 1966 the Cultural Revolution broke out in the People's Republic of China. The Red Guards of chairman Mao Zedong castigated the country and its inhabitants with juvenile impetuousness. A cruel war was waged against the "four old ones": old ideas, old cultures, old traditions, and old habits. Mahjong was judged to be part of the old ways. It was a gambling game and, as such, the officials warranted, a waste of time and an onset to corruption—thus it was considered an evil element that had to be exterminated. Indeed, the Chinese are quite fond of gambling and considerable amounts of money can be involved. A worker ought to spend his wage for his family and not on gambling, Mao said. The game was forbidden and trespassers were punished in public. In the opinion of the Chinese this was one of the biggest crimes of Mao. "If you wanted to play mahjong you had to hide like a villain," a mahjong veteran remembers. Nowhere else in the world is mahjong played with such enthusiasm as in China. Wherever a number of people is gathered together—whether for a wedding, a funeral, a birth, a meeting, or whatever—mahjong playing starts as soon as the official ceremonial part is concluded.

While mahjong was sentenced to death in the People's Republic, the game gained new popularity outside China, in Hong Kong, Taiwan, Japan, Vietnam, the Philippines, and Korea. Moreover, playing rules were adjusted to make the game younger, faster, and more exciting. In Hong Kong a simplified counting system was created, plus a way to play with twelve tiles. In Taiwan, where the game was also forbidden for a period, they started to play with sixteen tiles, and in Korea they began playing without the Bamboo suit. The new versions became very popular.

Nowadays Hong Kong is part of the People's Republic of China and the Red Guards have disappeared. Mao Zedong passed away in 1976. Mao was 70 percent right and 30 percent wrong, the Chinese now say, still trying to protect the dead leader's name, at least in part. What went wrong was mainly the fault of Jiang Qing, Mao's crazy wife, they also say. The sins of Mao are especially forgiven and forgotten since the ban on playing mahjong was lifted in 1998. Everywhere the mahjong tiles rattle: in the teahouses, in the public parks, or just at a plastic table on the sidewalk in the open air. And no one pays attention to the official playing rules, which were established by the Ministry of Sport Affairs and which forbid gambling most severely.

In the South-Chinese mountain village of Dali, four Chinese play their game of mahjong in the friendly surroundings of a public park.

The trade in mahjong sets tried eagerly to catch up with the losses incurred during the years that the game was banned. A new mahjong set costs about $20 in the Friendship store of Beijing. It contains sizeable tiles that are heavily painted and packed in a loud plastic box with a series of gilded characters on its cover. These tiles, which are sizeable enough to stand upright, are the most popular sets among the Chinese. Racks are not necessary. In the same store you can also find an ivory mahjong set for $6,000. The city of Chengdu in the Sichuan province is the mahjong Mecca. Day and night you hear mahjong tiles clattering everywhere. In the small street in front of the Wenshu Monastery, shop after shop displays mahjong sets in a dizzying assortment, priced at about $15. The backs of the tiles are made in the crudest colors, from garish pink to metallic orange. There are also felt mats for sale in all kinds of colors. These are used in the garden of the monastery where mahjong is played noiselessly at several tables with intense concentration. The tiles are not announced and the felt mats absorb the typical clattering sounds of the game as tiles are moved across the table. It is such a peaceful and cheerful sight that you cannot imagine that not so long ago Red Guards chased all mahjong players out of this garden and smashed their sets to pieces on command from the ever-smiling Mao Zedong.

Hong Kong

As a result of the mahjong ban, many Chinese forgot the traditional playing rules and switched to the modern versions, especially the Hong Kong version of mahjong. Notably the youngsters don't play anything else anymore. Hong Kong mahjong is the modern version of the elder Cantonese mahjong, which was popular after the Second World War. The mahjong idiom was then in Cantonese, while Hong Kong mahjong uses the more familiar Mandarin.

Lost a mahjong tile? There is a good chance that you will find a replacement in this basket in the shopping street of Chengdu. Otherwise, you can always buy a new mahjong set with a colorful assortment of tiles.

To avoid making blunders while playing with Chinese players here are the most important mahjong terms in the Cantonese and the Mandarin languages:

	Chow	Pung	Kong	mahjong
Cantonese	Sheung	Pung	Gong	sik
Mandarin	Chuh	Peng	Carng	hu

But ultimately what made Hong Kong mahjong very popular was its counting system. When playing Cantonese mahjong, scores increase linearly, but with

Hong Kong mahjong the increase is progressive. The Chinese like that. Also, outside China Hong Kong mahjong is well liked. Not only is it played everywhere in Asia, but it is fast gaining popularity in America and Europe.

Hong Kong mahjong knows two varieties: the Old Style and the New Style, which only differ in the scoring possibilities. The sober Old Style has a limited number of possibilities to score with Doubles; the New Style has an abundance of scoring combinations, which will be explained soon in "Combinations for Fan."

The most striking features of Hong Kong mahjong are:
- Only the winner scores;
- East does not pay double when he loses;
- Pungs and Kongs provide no points, but only Doubles (Fan);
- Bonus tiles may participate;
- The score is counted very fast; and
- A complete game is finished in a few hours.

Allocating Seats

Four different Wind tiles are mixed with the picture-side down and thereafter put in a neat row. An exposed 1-tile is added at one side and on the other side a 2-tile is added. It can also be an odd or an even tile.

Example: Someone has just thrown two or three dice. He counts the number of eyes and, in so doing, indicates the place where East will be seated. The player who is sitting there now throws the dice in his turn, this time to indicate the player who draws the first Wind tile. If the number of eyes is odd then the Wind tile has to be drawn from the side with the 1-tile (or odd tile); if it is even, then it is drawn from the other side. Thereafter the player to his right draws the next Wind tile, and so on. The player who drew East is going to sit at the place as indicated before by the dice. The rest sit in the order E-S-W-N, counterclockwise, based on the position of the East player.

Variant 1: The four Wind tiles are piled up. Odd or even is not taken into account. The rest of the procedure is the same.

Variant 2: The players decide who will become East, South, West, and North by drawing concealed Wind tiles. East may choose his seat at the table. The rest adjust. This variant is often used in the West where there is little sense of supernatural powers that decide the luck—good and bad—of the players.

If a complete game is played and the four players want to start a second game the dice are not used to pick who is East. East simply changes his seat with South, and West with North. The player who won the last hand becomes East.

Chips

Instead of bone sticks, brightly colored plastic coins serve to keep score. Here is a practical distribution of the coins:

Color	Value	Number	Total
Yellow	500	2	1000
Blue	100	9	900
Red	10	9	90
White	1	10	10
Total			2000

Whether you play for money or points, the chips can have another value:

Color	Value	Number	Total
Yellow	1000	4	4000
Blue	100	9	900
Red	10	9	90
White	2	5	10
Total			5000

When the scores become very high it is easier to use a notebook to keep track, because the counting is very simple. You write down the points of the winner and losers after each hand.

Building the Wall

The sides of the wall contain eighteen tiles because the bonus tiles are included. The tiles of the wall are not stacked on top of each other but put behind each other in two adjoining rows. The inside row is the "Upside." A tile is drawn first from that row and after that from the outside row.

The rows are laying side by side rather than one atop the other.

Variant: The wall is not built like a square, but like the blades of a windmill, which makes drawing the tiles easier. The walls are often very long because the game is played with extra large size tiles. The wall being used is constantly pushed toward the center of the table so the tiles are within reach of everyone.

Breaking the Wall

East decides which wall and in what place the wall will be broken. He throws three dice and counts up the thrown eyes, counterclockwise. Using that number he counts from right to left to the place on the wall where it has to be broken. No other players participate in the breaking of the wall.

East also sees to it that the dead wall has fourteen tiles.

The rows are placed like blades of a windmill.

Variant: Sometimes it is played without a dead wall and with all tiles being used. This variant is often agreed when the possibilities of winning are slight since only three or four Doubles are needed to go out.

Here are the number of eyes that determine which wall will be broken:

5	9	13	17	East
6	10	14	18	South
3	7	11	15	West
4	8	12	16	North

Fan

In Hong Kong mahjong no points are given to separate combinations or for the winning tile, and not even for a mahjong. Players only look at the number of Doubles in a winning hand. When added up, these Doubles give the number of Fan (pronounced *fa-an*) that your winning hand is worth. The minimum number of Fan to go mahjong is agreed to beforehand. That can be zero Fan, but most of the time the agreed upon minimum is 3 Fan. Bonus tiles are a helpful advantage in the latter because gathering 3 Fan is a difficult task.

In Hong Kong mahjong there is no difference between a Pung and a Kong (they are both worth nothing), and it only makes sense to Kong if you wish to have your turn earlier, or if you wish to draw the replacement tile for the chance of earning an extra Fan by completing your hand with a loose tile or with a Kong on Kong. It does not affect your score whether your Pung or Kong is exposed or not.

Only the winner's Fan are counted. The others can turn over their tiles immediately. The number of Fan decides how many points you receive from the others.

According to the table under "Fan and Points" on page 137, Fan are converted to points, but Chinese play for coins instead of for points. If you ever play Hong Kong mahjong with a Chinese player, inquire beforehand about what the limit is on the stake before you commit yourself to a game.

Because the number of Fan can increase considerably (and one plays for money in China) it became necessary to introduce a limit. The problem is immediately clear—with a simple, low limit nobody would be stimulated to go after big hands. Therefore increasing limits called Laak were invented; they simplify the counting even more and serve as maximums. Lots of adjustments can be made to the Laak, but the most common is to start with 4 Fan.

Therefore, a player who has more than 4 Fan reaches a 1 Laak limit. When you have 5 or 6 Fan the same limit applies. So it does not matter for your score if you have 4, 5, or 6 Fan. From 7 through 9 Fan the following limit applies: 2 Laaks. More than 10 Fan is the following and last limit: 3 Laaks. Usually this limit is not passed, although Chinese gamblers sometimes play until 20 Fan, equaling 5 Laaks, which produces a score of 2048 points (or yuan, or dollars). Sometimes the Laak system is not used at all so the scores can go up even more.

Winning and Losing

The goal in Hong Kong mahjong is to declare mahjong first. There is only one winner and only the winner scores. The way in which the winning tile was acquired determines who of the three losers has to pay.

- If the winner drew the winning tile from the wall all three losers pay him his score, so three times in total.
- If the winner took the winning tile from the table the player who discarded it has to pay the whole score of the winner and the other two players have each to pay half the score, so twice in total.

Variants: The player who discarded the winning tile pays the winner his whole score, twice his score, or three times his score if the discarded tile is claimed for a Kong and the winning tile is the loose tile.

Dangerous Discards

A player who carelessly discards the winning tile can bring much harm to the other players. In Hong Kong mahjong such a player can be punished because of risky play. This payment is called *pao*.

A discard is considered dangerous if:

- A player has three exposed combinations of one suit on the table. Someone who discards a tile that enables him to win with a Pure hand has to pay on behalf of all losers. This is called the Nine Tiles Penalty. There are some exceptions, which will be explained later on.
- The game is only five or less tiles away from a draw. If you now discard a tile

that was not discarded before and one of the players wins with this tile, you have to pay on behalf of all losers. This is called the Five Tiles Penalty.

• A player has three exposed Pungs/Kongs of Winds on the table. You discard one tile of the other Wind. If that player claims it to win with the special hand of Four Winds, you have to pay the winner twice his score.

• A player has two exposed Pungs/Kongs of Dragons on the table. You discard one tile of the other Dragon. If that player completes the Three Dragons (which earns 6 Fan) with your discard you have to pay on behalf of everybody.

• A player has three exposed Pungs/Kongs of Terminals on the table. You discard a Terminal. If that player completes All Terminals with your discard you have to pay the winner twice his score.

• A player has three exposed Pungs/Kongs Honor tiles on the table. You discard an Honor tile. If that player completes All Honors (worth 6 Fan) with your discard you have to pay on behalf of everybody.

Nine Tiles Penalty

If a player has exposed nine tiles of one suit it is considered a dangerous discard. If a player now discards a tile of the same suit and someone uses it to win a Pure hand, then the discarder has to pay for everyone. Even if the player does not win off the discarded tile, but only claims it to form a Pung, you will be held partially responsible.

Later, when that player draws the winning tile from the wall and reaches Pure hand, you have to pay on behalf of all players: so three times the score.

If you later discard the winning tile then you have to pay the winner twice his score. The other players don't pay anything.

If another player discards the winning tile, then he has to pay the winner on behalf of the others and you escape your penalty.

It can also occur that two players each have nine tiles of one suit exposed on the table. If you then have only tiles of dangerous suits, you have to discard the suit of the second dangerous hand to escape the penalty.

Example: South has three exposed Pungs of Characters on the table and later West has three exposed Pungs of Bamboos on the table. Two times dangerous play! North possesses only Characters and Bamboos in his hand. If he now discards a Character tile and South wins a Pure hand with it, North has to pay on behalf of the losers as well. Had North discarded a Bamboo tile and West won a Pure hand with it, North does not have to pay the others as well because it was the second dangerous hand. After the win North has to show his tiles to prove that there were no other tiles to discard safely.

Claiming the Winning Tile

A rule exists to reduce the risk of discarding a winning tile. If a Waiting Player did not claim the winning tile and afterward another player discards the same tile, he cannot claim that winning tile in the same turn. He can only claim such a tile when he has a turn again. It is always permitted to draw the winning tile from the wall.

Example: You have a Waiting Hand. The missing tile is 4-Bamboo. The player beside you discards 4-Bamboo. You hope for an extra Fan by drawing your winning tile from the wall and so you don't claim 4-Bamboo. Another player assumes that 4-Bamboo is a safe discard and throws a 4-Bamboo away. Your chance to draw that tile from the wall becomes considerably lessened. But, unfortunately, you are not allowed to claim the second 4-Bamboo. You have to draw a tile from the wall. If that tile turns out to be 4-Bamboo you will win with an extra Fan. However, it is not 4-Bamboo and you discard the tile. From that moment on you are allowed to claim 4-Bamboo again and go mahjong, as soon as the tile is discarded.

Penalties

Falsely claiming mahjong is punished. You have to pay every player 24 points. The game is over and a new hand starts. If East made the mistake, then the Wind changes as well.

Priority

If two or three players go out with the same discarded tile, then the player whose deal is first will have priority. An exception is made for the Thirteen Orphans. The player who can form this beautiful special hand always has priority.

Variant: You may agree in advance that when more players claim mahjong with the same discarded tile there will be more winners.

Fan and Points

Zero Fan is 4 points. 1 Fan is 8 points, 2 Fan is 16 points, and 3 Fan is 32 points. 4, 5, or 6 Fan is one Laak; 7, 8, or 9 Fan is 2 Laaks; 10 Fan is the limit and is 3 Laaks. Although it is not that complicated to calculate, Hong Kong mahjongers prefer to use a table in which everything is already calculated:

Fan	Laak	Winning tile discarded			Winning tile self-drawn	
		Winner	Discarder	Others	Winner	Others
0		+4	-2	-1		
1		+8	-4	-2	+12	-4
2		+16	-8	-4	+24	-8
3		+32	-16	-8	+48	-16
4, 5, 6	1	+64	-32	-16	+96	-32
7, 8, 9	2	+128	-64	-32	+192	-64
10 or more	3	+256	-128	-64	+384	-128

Example: You win with a discarded tile and 5 Fan. In the table you see that you scored 1 Laak, which is worth 64 points. The player who discarded your winning tile has to pay you 32 points, the other two pay you 16 points.

When you don't use chips you write +64 under your name, -32 under the discarder, and -16 under the other two names. The total is always 0.

Bonus Tiles

The bonus tiles can earn you Fan in the following ways:
• A hand without bonus tiles gives 1 Fan;
• Your own bonus tiles give 1 Fan;
• A series of all four flowers or seasons gives 1 Fan.
There are two series of bonus tiles that are called Head Seasons and Sub Seasons or seasons and gardens (or flowers). However, what is of importance is the prosaic number that is engraved beside the often very beautiful picture. Number 1 belongs to East, 2 to South, 3 to West, and 4 to North.

Often other agreements about the bonus tiles are made. Here are some possible variants:

- Every bonus tile or no bonus tiles at all give 1 Fan;
- The bonus tile of the prevailing Wind gives 1 Fan. For instance, when you pick bonus tile 2 in the south round, you earn 1 Fan;
- If your bonus tile is your own tile and the tile of the prevailing Wind, then it gives you 2 Fan. When you are, for instance, East in the first round, which is the East round, and you draw bonus tile 2, then you earn 2 Fan.
- If someone collects seven or eight bonus tiles he is automatically the winner.

Combinations for Fan

There are quite a few possibilities to collect Fan, especially with Hong Kong New Style. Because of the great number of combinations that brings Fan, this variant destroys the simplified play associated with Hong Kong mahjong. The following enumeration is not exhaustive, and yet it is still quite long.

You can make a choice from this list for your own house rules.

Chicken Hand	0	

A hand consisting of ordinary Chows, Pungs, and a pair.

All Chows	1	
Concealed hand	1	

The winning tile may be a discarded tile. This hand is called "clear front door."

Winning tile is self-drawn	1	
Winning with last tile for a draw	1	
Winning with a loose tile	1	

Attention: You also get 1 Fan if the winning tile is self-drawn.

Pung of Dragons	1	
Pung of own Wind	1	
Pung of prevailing Wind	1	
No bonus tiles	1	

Own bonus tile	1	
Prevailing bonus tile	1	
Pair of 2, 5, or 8	1	New style
Chow 1-2-3 and 7-8-9 of same suit	1	New style

This combination is also known as "young and old."

Corresponding Chows		New style

The Chinese call this kind of combination "nephews."

Two suits	1	New style

A hand of only two suits and Honor tiles.

Little Four-in-One	1	New style

Four matching tiles: three in a Pung and one in a Chow.

Two same Chows in one suit	2	New style

For instance, two Chows of Characters 2-3-4. This is known as "sisters."

Four-in-One	2	New style

Four matching tiles: two in Chows and two in a pair.

Exposed Twelve	2	New style

You have twelve tiles exposed and with the one tile on your rack you form the winning pair.

Exposed Snake	2	New style

Three succeeding Chows 1-2-3, 4-5-6, and 7-8-9, one of which is exposed

All Pungs/Kongs	3	
Cleared Hand	3	
Series of bonus tiles	3	

Bonus tiles 1 through 4 of one suit: so, all four seasons, all four flowers, or any complete series.

Concealed Snake	3	New style

Three succeeding Chows 1-2-3, 4-5-6, and 7-8-9, all concealed.

Five Doors	3	New style

A hand composed of all the different types of tiles: Characters, Bamboos, Circles, Winds, and Dragons.

Only tiles 1 through 5	3	New style
Five Corners	3	New style

Terminals in every combination.

All discards	3	New style

No concealed combinations: all combinations were claimed.

All tiles 3 through 7	3	New style
All tiles 5 through 9	3	New style
Kong on Kong	4	

You form a Kong and pick a loose tile from the dead wall. With this tile you make another Kong and with the second loose tile you obtain mahjong.

All pairs	4	
Little Three Dragons	4	

Two Pungs of Dragons and a Pair of Dragons.

| Little Four Winds | 4 | |

Three Pungs of Winds and a Pair of Winds.

| Succeeding Pungs | 4 | New style |

Three succeeding Pungs of one suit, for instance:

| Matching Pungs | 4 | New style |

Matching Pungs in three suits, for instance:

| Three Dragons | 6 | |

Three Pungs of Dragons. This hand is not regarded as a special hand in Hong Kong New Style.

| Three same Chows | 6 | New style |

| Big Four-in-One | 6 | New style |

Four matching tiles in four Chows, for instance:

| Pure hand | 6 | |
| One number | 6 | New style |

Same number in every combination, for instance:

Three numbers	6	New style

Only three numbers in your hand, for instance:

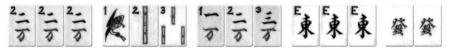

All Honors	7	

This is not a special hand in Hong Kong New Style.

Thirteen Orphans	limit

One each of Honors and Terminals and one tile Double.

Concealed Treasure	limit

Four concealed Pungs (no Kongs). The winning tile completes a pair and is self-drawn.

All Terminals	limit

Pungs/Kongs of Terminals.

Nine Gates	limit
Heaven's Blessing	limit
Earth's Blessing	limit

Mahjong with 12 tiles

Everything is possible in mahjong, including playing with twelve tiles. This is an exciting variant of Hong Kong mahjong, but it can be used with every kind of mahjong. The thirteenth missing tile is an invisible Joker, which can replace any tile. You declare mahjong with thirteen tiles and by announcing which invisible tile is the missing tile from your hand. In this way the chance of going mahjong is increased considerably and the skill level is much more complex.

Matches as Chips

Every Chinese has to see once in his lifetime the Three Pagodas at the Er Hai Lake. That is why the site bustles with day-trippers and ships come and go on the lake. Some ships are built like real dragons. The guide, who pulls you on board with his right hand, carries a plastic bag in his left hand. Once floating on the hazy lake he shakes out the contents of the bag over a small flowery blanket. There appear 136 mahjong tiles. You cannot let such a chance slide away and within a short time an impromptu international game is being played.

Rather than bone tallies, matches serve as chips. Officially mahjong is not allowed to be played for money. Therefore settling occurs discreetly afterward. Sometimes cigarettes serve as chips. These are not converted into coins.

It became a big victory for the two Europeans on board. Our Chinese opponents smiled politely but seemed a little dazed. They would forget to settle so we would have matches for days and days. During the rest of our trip we were always greeted with a broad smile and treated with courtesy; we were no longer just anonymous outsiders. The connections made with others while playing mahjong are worth as much as the pleasure taken in winning it.

A blanket serves as a table in this impromptu game of mahjong.

Example:

Your hand consists of two Chows of Characters and a series of Bamboos. It is a Waiting Hand with several possibilities to go mahjong, six in total.

With a 1-Bamboo:

The tile with the red border is the winning tile; the tile with the blue border is the invisible Joker.

With a 2-Bamboo:

With a 3-Bamboo:

With a 4-Bamboo:

With a 5-Bamboo:

With a 6-Bamboo:

It is very nice to have four combinations of three tiles. Every tile is then a winning tile because the invisible Joker completes it as a pair:

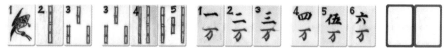

Mahjong with Sixteen Tiles

This remarkable variant originated in Taiwan and is therefore named Taiwanese mahjong as well, although it is also played in the Philippines. To declare mahjong you have to complete five combinations of three tiles and a pair. Because you play with many tiles the score can run up considerably. Also, here it is not the value of the combinations that is so important, but the number of Doubles. You say "Tai" instead of Fan.

Seating Arrangements

The players are sitting at random around the table. Four different Wind tiles are piled up. One of the players throws the dice. The seat of the thus indicated player will become the seat of the temporary East Wind. The indicated player also throws the dice, now to indicate the player who has to draw the upper Wind tile. The player to his right draws the second, and so on. Temporary East is seated at the indicated chair and the others take their positions.

Hereafter the wall is built, eighteen tiles long, because the bonus tiles also participate.

The player indicated as temporary East throws the two dice and in this way determines which player will start the game as East and which wall has to be opened. The number of eyes also determines where the wall will be opened, counted from right to left.

Variant: If the player throws a double then the hand will be played for double points.

The players draw four tiles in turns, for a total of four turns each. Bonus tiles are exposed and replaced in turns by loose tiles from the dead wall. Only after this is done does East draw his seventeenth tile. If East loses he pays one Tai extra, if he wins he receives one Tai extra. He remains East and receives two extra Tai for each time he keeps his position.

The dead wall counts sixteen tiles, just like in Old-Chinese mahjong. Usually the dead wall consists of fourteen tiles.

The Game

The great number of tiles offers a variety of possibilities for play, and at the same time requires optimal concentration. The usual special hands are impossible to obtain because they are based on fourteen tiles, excluding Heaven's Blessing and Earth's Blessing. Obtaining a Pure hand is extremely difficult and receives the highest reward, 40 Tai, the same as for Heaven's or Earth's Blessing.

The limit is usually 300 Tai, with 600 Tai for East. The minimal number of Tai needed to go mahjong is agreed upon before the game starts. Five Tai is customary.

Secret Kong

The Kong is always kept concealed, even when it is placed on the table. This keeps the identity of the tiles a secret, as the Filipinos say. Cheating is not possible because the Kong has to be revealed afterward. Making a Kong is difficult because fourteen tiles less are discarded.

Filipinos like to play for money, which is settled immediately. For an exposed Kong you get 25¢ from all other players, and 50¢ for a concealed Kong. A Tai earns usually 5¢.

Combinations for Tai

Here are the possibilities for scoring points:

Mahjong	2
Bonus tile	1
No bonus tiles	1
Honor tile	1
No Honor tiles	1
No Terminals	1
All Chows	1

Winning with self-drawn	1
Exposed Kong	1
Robbing a Kong	1
Winning with the last tile before a draw	1
Winning with a loose tile	1
All concealed	1
Pung of Dragons	1
Pung of own Wind	1
Pung of prevailing Winds	1
Concealed Kong	2
Winning with a pair	2
Only Possible Place	2
All concealed, winning tile included	3
Winning before 10 tiles are discarded	3
Three concealed Pungs	5
Snake with one or more Pungs exposed	5
Two Pungs of Winds and a pair of Winds	5
Cleared Hand	10
All Pungs	10
Concealed Snake	10
No bonus tiles and no Honors	10
Exposed hand and winning tile is self-drawn	10
Winning before 5 tiles are discarded	10
Little Three Dragons	15
Winning after announcing a Waiting Hand in first turn	15
Three Pungs of Winds	15
Four concealed Pungs	15
Possessing 7 bonus tiles and robbing the eighth	20
All the bonus tiles	30
Little Four Winds	30
Three Dragons	30
Seven pairs and a concealed Pung	30
Four Winds	40
Pure hand	40

Heaven's Blessing	40
Earth's Blessing	40
Five concealed Pungs	40

Mahjong with Two Suits

In Korean mahjong Bamboo tiles aren't used, and so it is played with two instead of three suits. Therefore it is very suited for three players instead of four. Also, creating more complicated hands is easier.

Other Features

An exposed Chow is not permitted. Chows can only be formed with tiles drawn from the wall.

You are not allowed to win with a tile you discarded before. Therefore you cannot discard your tiles randomly within the wall, but you have to discard them in neat rows in front of you, so it is always clear which tiles you possessed.

You play with 104 tiles: the Characters, the Circles, the Winds, the Dragons and four bonus tiles.

To win you need a minimum of 2 Fan. All Chows, All Simples, a Pung of Dragons, or a Pung of your own Wind is rewarded with 1 Fan. You can also earn 1 Fan with a concealed hand and with a discarded winning tile. An all concealed hand (also winning tile) gives you 2 Fan. That applies also to Cleared-Hand and All Pungs. The Little Three Dragons, Seven Pairs, and Three concealed Pungs are worth 3 Fan. Little Four Winds, Pure hand, Three Dragons, All Terminals, and Four concealed Pungs get 8 Fan. You get 12 Fan for Four Winds and All Honors and 16 Fan for Heaven's or Earth's Blessing. Nine Gates is rewarded with 24 Fan. These are the basic Fan. In addition, you can earn 1 extra Fan for every bonus tile, winning with the last tile before a draw (5 or 8 Fan when it is 1-Circles). Winning with a Kong gives you 5 or 8 Fan when it is 5-Circles, Robbing a Kong gives you 5 Fan, and four bonus tiles give you 8 Fan.

The winning tile becomes automatically a premium tile. Every premium tile earns you 1 extra Fan. Therefore going mahjong always gives you 1 to 4 extra Fan.

Example: You win by completing a Pung of 6-Circles. So 6-Circles is the premium tile. Thus you have 3 premium tiles and you receive 3 extra Fan. If you also have a Chow with 6-Circles in it then you receive 4 extra Fan in total.

If you win with a pair of 3-Characters, then you receive 2 extra Fan. For every 3-Character in your hand you get 1 extra Fan.

A complete game consists of eight Winds, a minimum of thirty-two hands.

Variant: There is no end to the game. The player who won becomes East. This continues until the time is over, you run out of money, there is no more liquid refreshment, or any other reason.

After a draw every player puts a chip of 1 Fan inside the wall. These chips are destined for the player who goes mahjong with a concealed hand. After the game comes to a draw three times in a row the players take back their chips and donate one new chip to the kitty.

If you have a completely concealed Waiting Hand you may announce it, like in Riichi mahjong. If you win, you get 2 extra Fan. The winning hand must bring in the necessary minimum Fan. If you announce that you are going to win with a self-drawn tile, then you collect 3 extras Fan when you succeed.

Making completely concealed hands (including the winning tile) is encouraged with "kyung-ma," the horse race. At the beginning of the game all players receive three separate chips, which they put on the table faceup. If a player finishes with a concealed hand, he removes one of his chips. The player who removes his chips first wins the horse race and receives 2 Fan from all players. Players who have not completed at least one concealed hand by that time have to pay double—4 Fan. All players reset their three chips and a new horse race begins.

Chinese Official International Rules

In October 2002 the first world-championship mahjong tournament took place in Tokyo, jointly organized by Japan and China. It was a remarkable event in more than one way. Only four years prior mahjong was strictly forbidden in the Chinese People's Republic. But by the time of the tournament new playing rules had been collected and defined on command of the Chinese government. With this immense undertaking Beijing sought to redeem itself for having cruelly banned the favorite Chinese pastime and for having punished trespassers severely. Trumpeting the new "noble" mahjong, Chinese rulers now spoke of "clean" games since gambling was virtually eradicated, at least officially.

No longer merely a game, mahjong is now recognized by China as an official sport with official regulations defined by the official State Sports Commission. The new sport is so ordered and sportsmanlike that smoking or shouting is not permitted during playing. And gambling—the national weakness—is absolutely forbidden. Just like any other sport, mahjong's sole goal is to elevate body and spirit. When the Communist party members experimented with the new mahjong rules in utmost secrecy they had to swear solemnly that they would play "obediently, gracefully, nobly, and honestly." The Chinese rulers wanted to regain international respect with their new "healthy" and "hygienic" mahjong rules, and at this they seemed to be successful.

These rules, which are becoming very popular at international contests, are also called "Official Mahjong" and "Peking Mahjong."

Not only was the world championship of 2002 played under these rules, but also the open championships of China afterward and the first open European championship of 2005 in Holland.

Striking features of the Chinese official international mahjong rules are:
- No limit to points;
- Deals continue always, even after East wins or after a draw;
- Minimum of 8 points to go out; and
- No dead wall.

The bonus tiles (flowers) participate. All bonus tiles are equal and worth 1 point but these points don't count for the minimum 8 points needed to go out. You don't have to claim a bonus tile immediately but can wait until a more suitable moment.

Discarded tiles are placed in front of a player in orderly rows of six, from left to right, so everyone can verify the tiles and the order in which they were disposed.

Only the winner scores. If his winning tile was self-drawn the winner receives his score plus 8 points from each of the three other players. If the winning tile was discarded the winner receives 8 points from his three opponents as well as payment of his score by the discarder.

A hand may contain a number of scoring combinations. The winner adds all his scoring combinations together for his total of points.

This hand has several scoring combinations: Big Three Dragons, All Terminals and Honors and One Voided Suit; 88 + 32 + 1 = 121 points.

You always have to declare the highest scoring possible, because lower scoring hands are included in the higher scoring hands. Big Three Dragons includes Little Three Dragons, three concealed Pungs includes two concealed Pungs, and so on. Any combination that is included in an already scored combination does not earn additional points. Note also that your combinations are irreversible. Pure Triple Chow may not be counted as Pure shifted Pungs as well. You have to choose between the two possibilities.

Many Patterns

Chinese official international mahjong is strongly focused on the numbers of the tiles. With these numbers patterns are formed, which lead to new and surprising possibilities. Many combinations involve shifted Chows, or three or more Chows offset by a consistent number of tiles (either two or three depending on the hand), and sometimes you will even see, although less commonly, shifted Pungs or three or more Pungs that are in succession (either in the same suit, or one of each, such as a Pung of 3-Bamboos, a Pung of 4-Characters, and a Pung of 5-Circles).

Shifted Chows of one suit—the left ones each shifted with two tiles, the right ones with one tile. Shifted Chows and Pungs must always have three combinations.

Eighty-One Combinations

To become a champion you have to master the following eighty-one combinations. Like menus in a Chinese restaurant, the combinations are identified with numbers (in the second column) that make it easier for you to communicate with your competitors and the referees.

Types of Wait

Edge-Wait—going out on 3 or 7 when holding 1-2 or 8-9	9	1
Closed Wait—going out on middle tile of a Chow	10	1
Single Wait—going out on a pair	11	1
Self-Drawn—going out on a tile from the wall	12	1
Concealed Hand—and going out with a discarded tile	17	2
Fully concealed Hand—and going out with a self-drawn tile	25	4
Last Tile—going out with last tile of its kind when first three tiles are on table	27	4
Melded Hand—going out with an exposed pair with a fully exposed hand	32	6
Last Tile Draw—going out by drawing the last tile of the game	40	8
Last Tile Claim—going out with last discard of the game	41	8
Out with Replacement Tile	42	8
Robbing the Kong	43	8

Chows

Chows earn no points, but combinations of Chows do. Chow hands, formed by only Chows, may not include a pair of Honor tiles.

Chow Hands

Pure Double Chow	1	1
Mixed Double Chow	2	1
All Chows	18	2
Mixed Triple Chow—three same numerical sequences	37	8
Pure Triple Chow—three same numerical sequences of same suit	59	24
Quadruple Chow—four same numerical sequences of same suit	67	48

Straight Hands

Short Straight—two Chows of one suit with increasing numbers	3	1
Mixed Straight—tiles 1-9 in Chows of all three suits	35	8
Knitted Straight—see also Knitting (page 154)	45	12
Pure Straight—tiles 1-9 in Chows of one suit	49	16

Terminal Hands

Two Terminal Chows—two Chows including 1 and 9 in one suit	4	1
Three-suited Terminal Chow—1-2-3 + 7-8-9 in two suits, 5-5 in third suit	50	16
Pure Terminal Chow—1-2-3, 1-2-3, 7-8-9, 7-8-9, 5-5 in one suit	74	64

Step-up Hands

Mixed shifted Chows—three Chows, each shifted one tile up from last	30	6
Pure shifted Chows—three Chows, each shifted one or two tiles up from the last	51	16
Four shifted Chows—four Chows, each shifted one tile up from the last	64	32

Pungs and Kongs

For ordinary Pungs you do not get points, but you do for Kongs.

Pung Hands

Pung of Terminals or Honors	5	1
Double Pung	20	2
Two concealed Pungs	21	2
All Pungs	28	6
Mixed shifted Pungs—three Pungs each shifted up in three suits	38	8
Triple Pung—three Pungs of same number in three suits	53	16
Three concealed Pungs	54	16

All Even—only even numbers in all combinations	57	24
Pure shifted Pungs—three Pungs each shifted up in one suit	60	24
All Terminals and Honors	66	32
Four Pure shifted Pungs—four Pungs each shifted up in one suit	68	48
All Terminals	69	64
Four concealed Pungs	73	64

Kong Hands

Melded Kong	6	1
Concealed Kong	22	2
Two melded Kongs	26	4
Melded Kong and concealed Kong	26a	6
Two concealed Kongs	33	8
Three Kongs	65	32
Four Kongs	79	64

Honors

Pung of Dragons	14	2
Pung of prevailing Winds	15	2
Pung of own Winds	16	2
Two Pungs of Dragons	34	6
Big Three Winds	48	12
Little Four Winds	70	64
Little Three Dragons	71	64
All Honors	72	64
Big Four Winds	75	88
Big Three Dragons	76	88

Numbers

All Simples	23	2
Outside Hand—Terminals or Honors in all combinations	24	4
Upper Four—only tiles from 6 through 9	46	12
Lower Four—only tiles from 1 through 4	47	12
All Fives—a tile -5 in every combination	52	16
Upper Tiles—only tiles -7, -8, and -9	61	24
Middle Tiles—only tiles -4, -5, and -6	62	24
Lower Tiles—only tiles -1, -2, and -3	63	24

Suits

One Voided Suit—one suit is missing	7	1
No Honors	8	1
Half Flush—Clean hand	29	6
All Types—a hand composed of all different types of tiles	31	6
Full Flush—Pure hand	58	24
All Green	77	88
Nine Gates	78	88

Nine Gates

A Pung of 1s, a sequence of 2 through 8, and a Pung of 9s, all in one suit. The winning tile is a Double tile.

This fine hand derives its name from its exceptional structure. With 1-1-1 2-3-4-5-6-7-8 9-9-9 waiting on your rack, you can obtain a regular mahjong with any of the nine tiles of that suit.

A 1 results namely in: Pung 1-1-1, Chows 1-2-3, 4-5-6, 7-8-9, and a Pair 9-9.

A 2 results in: Pung 1-1-1, Pair 2-2, Chows 3-4-5, 6-7-8, and Pung 9-9-9.

A 3 results in: Pair 1-1, Chows 1-2-3, 3-4-5, 6-7-8, and Pung 9-9-9.

Thus there are nine gates to a mahjong.

Knitting

Knitted Straight	45	12
Lesser Honors and Knitted tiles	44	12
Greater Honors and Knitted tiles	56	24

Knitting is an attractive way of going out. Knitted tiles consist of tiles 1-4-7, 2-5-8, and 3-6-9 in different suits.

Three Knitted Chows are called Knitted Straight (45 points).

The three Knitted Chows are part of a winning hand. Its value depends on the two other combinations. If those are an arbitrary Pung and a pair, you can only claim Knitted Straight (45), which gives you 12 points. If those are a Pung of Dragons (14) and All Types (31—at least if you have a pair of Winds), which gives you 12 + 2 + 6 = 20 points. If the two other combinations are an arbitrary Chow and an arbitrary pair you can claim All Chows (18) as well and earn 12 + 2 = 14 points.

When the rest of your hand consists of only single Honor tiles you can claim Lesser Honors and Knitted Tiles (44), which gives you 12 points.

If the rest of your hand consists of all seven Honor tiles, it will appear as though you are in trouble because in that instance you cannot have three Knitted Chows. But curiously enough you now have reached Greater Honors and Knitted Tiles (56) and earn 24 points. In this case you don't need a complete Knitted Straight. Even more curious is that when you have neither a complete Knitted Straight nor all 7 Honors, you can claim Lesser Honors and Knitted Tiles and so earn 12 points.

A hand formed by seven single Honor tiles and suit tiles belonging to separate knitted sequences (1-, 4-, 7-Bamboo, 2-, 5-, 8-Character, 3-, 6-, 9-Circles). It is called Greater Honors and Knitted Tiles and brings in 24 points.

Pairs

All Pairs	55	24
Shifted Pairs	80	88

Seven pairs of the same suit, each shifted one up from the last

When you win with All Pairs extra points are possible for Half Flush (29), All Types (31), One Voided Suit (7), and Tile Hog (19).

Special Hands

Flower tile	13	1
Tile Hog—all four same tiles and no Kong declared	19	2

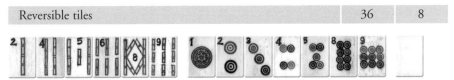

Using all four of a single suit without declaring them as a Kong. 2-Character is used four times in this hand.

Reversible tiles	36	8

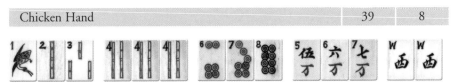

2-, 4-, 5-, 6-, 8- and 9-Bamboo, 1-, 2-, 3-, 4-, 5-, 8- and 9-Circles plus the White Dragon are the reversible tiles. It does not matter how you place these tiles, they always look the same since they are vertically symmetrical (without the Arabic numerals).

Chicken Hand	39	8

A hand that would otherwise earn no points. All combinations have no value.

Thirteen Orphans	81	88

Fortune Telling

Mahjong tiles are used by Chinese fortune-tellers to predict the future. They arrange all the mahjong tiles in a magic mahjong square. The Chinese like to consult soothsayers for all kind of affairs, and a visit to the temple is not complete without such a consultation. Fortune-tellers are held in high esteem and their predictions are regarded seriously. Most fortune-tellers use wooden blocks or numbered bamboo sticks, but the highest level of fortune-telling, called Ya Pai Shen Ho, divines with ivory blocks. These blocks can be dominoes or mahjong tiles. Mahjong tiles, however, are more suited for detailed work, because there are four and a half more mahjong tiles than dominoes. The future can be interpreted with much more nuance and insight.

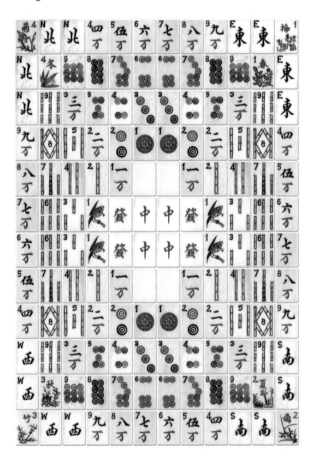

GREAT BRITAIN

The first European addicted to mahjong was probably the Englishman L. L. Harr. He traveled in the intellectual and diplomatic circles in Peking and among his friends was the distinguished Chinese statesman Li Hung Chang. One night that he would not easily forget, Li showed the Englishman a set that consisted of soft shining ivory tiles, clearly painted with miniatures of bamboos, birds, dragons, and other figures. The Chinese called the game "Pe-ling" and according to Li Hung, it was centuries and centuries old.

For two years, Harr played the fascinating game with his Chinese friend before he returned to Europe in 1921, traveling by ship from Bombay to Marseilles. In his luggage were five sets of the game. The ship had hardly left Bombay when Harr made a wager with three English whist enthusiasts. Harr asserted that before they reached Marseilles all passengers on board would only want to play his new game. The three whist players lost their bet resoundingly because even before the ship reached Aden nothing else was played on board besides "Pe-ling." When the ship finally moored in Marseilles, Harr had to hurry to telegraph a friend in China for eighty new sets to satisfy the demands of his

The English aristocracy enjoyed itself supremely with the new exotic game. One tournament followed another, the last one still more decadent than the one before. A wealthy American tried to exceed them all by adding a special mahjong hall with a vault of big mahjong tiles to his country house. But that was a lack of good taste, the English aristocrats judged.

fellow passengers. With only one set still in his possession, he traveled to London. "And so the game was, I believe, first introduced to London society," according to Harr.

It was only a few years later when J. P. Babcock introduced the same game in England, but with a different name, "Mah-Jongg," and with other, much simpler rules. "It is not the magnificent game I learned from Li Hung Chang," lamented Harr. "It's lacking all the qualities that make it so interesting and it is degraded to a childish and dull game." He started a campaign against Babcock's rules, preaching the rules of mahjong as he learned from his famous Chinese friend.

The Court Mahjongs, Too

The London nobility were delighted by the game, and the more exotic the rules became the more thrilling the pleasure. Even the royal court became absorbed in mahjong, Princess Mary especially. Prince George had to play the game, too, after the Queen presented him with a mahjong set for his birthday. In the chic mahjong club at Hans Road, four female members of high society dressed up in Chinese garments and locked themselves behind doors to play the Game of the Hundred Wonders for twelve successive hours. They did not stop for meals or even for tea. Every hour a bulletin on the progress of the game was posted on the closed doors. The Spanish queen sent an envoy to Hans Road to ask for rules and an explanation of the game. Chinese diplomats were constantly hounded by mahjong fanatics to join them at the table for a game. One of them answered with diplomatic tact that although he had already studied the game for ten years, he still needed at least five more years to master it. This diplomatic answer only added to the exoticism of mahjong, increasing the hype surrounding the game even more.

Mahjong Silk Stockings

The London fashion world took advantage of the craze and launched silken ladies' stockings decorated with symbols from the game. The stockings were woven of dark silk and, between knee and ankle, were odd appliqués of mahjong pictures that, as a newspaper reporter wrote indignantly, "as a matter of fact belonged nowhere else than at the playing table and, well, on the tiles, which form the Chinese wall." The decoration was applied differently on each stocking, reported the same writer. "The left leg bears the sign of 1-Bamboo (the bird), and the right leg is decorated with Dragon and flower, with Wind or Character."

The newest fashion—stockings decorated with mahjong symbols

Mahjong Holes

Mahjong clubs especially flourished in the Chinese quarters of cities like London and Liverpool, and it was not only the nobility that visited them. Newspaper reporters in 1924 wrote therefore contemptuously of "mahjong holes":

> There, in the quarters where the sin governs and decay spreads around, there the mahjong lovers come to visit the mahjong parlours. Chattering Chinese, white persons from all layers of the society, sailors, prize fighters, but also ladies and gentlemen from society, people who are looking for that new sensation, young bloods searching adventure—all those you will find there. And also many ladies from the London West End come to this place to celebrate their passion for mahjong. A wide sample-card of fortune seekers, villains, and bohemians is seen in the mahjong parlours. And by far not all those unbalanced peoples, who wind up here, end up without mental or material damage. Many ladies who came looking for sensation in these places of doom, have become victims of blackmailers who threaten to reveal their nightly excursions, when a silence cannot be bought.

Playing Rules

Nowadays mahjong in England is as respected as the quintessential British gentleman. The British Mah-Jong Association guards over the regulations, organizes tournaments, and acts as a referee in disputes.

Aspects of the British rules are:
- Bonus tiles participate,
- Joker tiles participate in the Goulash,
- Only one Chow is allowed,
- Announcing a Waiting Hand is obligatory,
- Goulash after a draw, and
- Penalties for mistakes.

Pow!
Building the wall also works a bit differently. Two players (mostly South and North, but never East) mix the tiles until East judges that they have been shuffled sufficiently and calls "Pow." The four players then build a wall that is eighteen tiles long because the bonus tiles are used.

Dead Wall
The dead wall, also called "Kong Box," is not replenished to maintain fourteen tiles, but becomes shorter and shorter.

Only One Chow
You can use all suits to go out. The only restriction is that your mahjong may contain not more than one Chow.

Announcing Waiting Hand
Instead of a Waiting Hand the British speak of a Fishing Hand. You are obliged to announce it, otherwise you cannot claim mahjong. In this way, the other players are warned and they will be extra careful when they discard a tile.

Goulash after a Draw
When no one reaches mahjong, a Goulash follows. The four 2-Bamboo tiles are replaced by Joker tiles, which may represent any other tile. If the set does not have Joker tiles then the four 2-Bamboos act as Jokers.

The tiles are mixed, the wall is built again, and the tiles are drawn. The players then select three of their most unwanted tiles, place them facedown on the table, and change them with their opposite player. After that they again select three unwanted tiles, lay them facedown on the table, and change them with the player to the right. The third and last time the change is made with the player to the left.

After the Goulash, no Chow at all is allowed, except when they are part of a special hand.

Penalties

When you make mistakes, which can harm the other players, you are penalized.

- If you have a Dead Hand with too few tiles, you have to continue but you are not allowed to go out. You may, however, Chow, Pung, or Kong as long as you have a tile left to discard. You may count your score and settle it with the other players.
- If you have a Dead Hand with too many tiles, you have to continue but may not go out or count your score.
- If you name a discarded tile wrongly and a player claims the called tile for a Chow, Pung, or Kong, then you have to pay him 50 points. When the called tile is claimed for mahjong, then that tile applies as the winning tile and the hand stops. You have to pay the winner also on behalf of the other two players. The other players do not settle their scores.
- When you falsely announce mahjong and nobody has exposed his hand, the play goes on and there is no penalty for the player who called in error. However, when a player has exposed his hand, you have to pay the other three players a half-limit score.
- If you mistakenly claim a discarded tile, you are allowed to undo your error before the turn moves on. If the turn is over, you may not correct your mistake. The erroneous combination remains on the table, the play goes on, but you may not go mahjong.
- If you discard a tile that the Waiting Player can use for going out, you are punished severely. This is called dangerous play. You have to pay the winner on behalf of the others and moreover pay the two losers their scores. Nothing further is settled.

Dangerous play applies:

- When there are nine exposed tiles of one suit in front of a player with a Waiting Hand and you discard a tile of the same suit;
- When a Waiting Player has three exposed Pungs of Winds and you discard a fourth Wind tile;
- If a Waiting Player has two exposed Pungs of Dragons and you discard a third Dragon;
- When a Waiting Player has three exposed Pungs of Terminals and you discard a Terminal tile; and
- When a Waiting Player has three exposed Pungs of Green Bamboos and you discard another Green Bamboo.

Settling Points

The value of the tiles is the same as in basic mahjong but there are differences in the appreciation of a number of hands. The British don't give points for Only Possible Tile and for completing a pair.

Doubling is almost the same as in basic mahjong:

Pung/Kong of Dragons	1 x
Pung/Kong of prevailing Winds	1 x
Pung/Kong of own Wind	1 x
All Pungs	1 x
Fully concealed hand	1 x
Cleared hand—one suit with Honors	1 x
All Honors and Terminals	1 x
Winning with a loose tile	1 x
Winning with the last tile from the wall	1 x
Winning with the last discarded tile	1 x
Winning with the original thirteen tiles	1 x
Robbing a Kong	1 x
Purity—only one suit and no Chows	3 x

Bonus tiles:

Own flower	1 x
Own season	1 x
All flowers	2 x
All seasons	2 x

There are eighteen special hands. The limit is generally 1000 points. A Waiting ("fishing") Special Hand receives two-fifths of the limit, so 400 points. There are some special hands you haven't seen until now.

Twisting Snake

A pair of 1s, a sequence from 2 to 9 of the same suit, and one of every Wind. Except for the winning tile, it has to be concealed.
Score: limit.

Note: This hand should not be confused with the Wriggling Snake and the Wriggly Snake. Typically the "head" of the snake is two tiles long.

All Honor Pairs

Seven pairs of only Honor tiles.
Score: half limit.
All Honor pairs are the only permitted Twin Hands in Great Britain.

Buried Treasure

Only Pungs and a pair of one suit, with Winds and Dragons.
It should be played completely concealed.
Score: limit.

Note: This hand is not the same as Concealed Hand, in which you are allowed to use all suits.

Plucking the Moon from the Bottom of the Sea

You win with the last tile of the wall that you draw yourself, before it becomes a draw, and this last tile is 1-Circle (the "moon"). You score the limit.

When it is the last tile and self-drawn, 1-Circle gives this winning hand three extra doubles. If North is the prevailing Wind you can receive five and even six doubles.

Gathering the Plum Blossom from the Roof

You make a Kong and so you draw a tile from the dead wall. If this is 5-Circles (the "plum blossom") and it is your winning tile, you score the limit.

Nine Gates

A Pung of 1s, a Pung of 9s, a sequence of 2 through 8, and a tile Double: all in one suit.

Except in Chinese official mahjong there are no restrictions for the winning tile. Any tile that completes this exceptional hand will do.

The other eleven special hands are:

Knitting	half limit	Three Dragons	limit
Triple Knitting	half limit	Four Winds	limit
Imperial Jade	limit	Kong on Kong	limit
Thirteen Orphans	limit	Heaven's Blessing	limit
Four Kings	limit	Earth's Blessing	limit
Heads and Tails	limit		

Tournaments

In tournaments in Great Britain the following exceptions apply:

- The bonus tiles do not participate;
- There is no Goulash—after a draw the game will just start again;
- It is forbidden to win three times in a row with the same special hand.

Mahjong Calculator

The mahjong calculator was introduced around 1925 to help with the sometimes laborious calculations. First you had to turn the disc in such a way that the number 0 appeared in the round red cubbyhole to the left (the "Hand Value"). After that it was easy to calculate and to double your score.

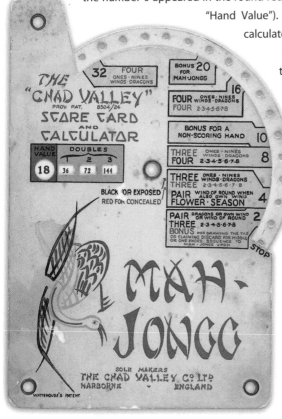

For instance, if you had three exposed Dragons you would first look for the black printed line "Three Ones Nines Winds Dragons," then you stuck the point of a pencil in the corresponding cubby hole and turned the disc until it stopped. You repeated this for every combination and after that you could read under the Hand Value your points total and under Doubles your doubled points. The doubles from 4 to 7 are printed on the backside.

HOLLAND

Early in 1923 a certain J. P. from Amsterdam inquired of the editor of a Dutch news magazine "if the Chinese game Mah-Jongg, which as he understood has been played for hundreds of years in China, is also known in Europe." The editor was not familiar with the game. "It should be a game of ivory and bone tiles, on which Chinese symbols are engraved, looking somewhat like dominoes," he declared, but the game was not yet known in Holland. "Does one of our readers know where this game is possibly available?" the editor of the magazine asked.

The 1924 December catalogue from Perry's department store was filled with mahjong articles, from a 25¢ calculator to sets in five-drawer boxes for $30 or more.

The firm Perry & Co. in Amsterdam took the challenge immediately. The department store had good connections in the United States and always sold the newest American products in its Dutch branches. Before Joseph Babcock discovered Holland on the world map, the new game was already displayed in the windows of Perry. "Mah Jongg is a centuries-old game, brought to perfection in a game of delicacy, calculation, and logic," so the firm introduced the new game. "Mah Jongg is easy enough to learn, but only after much playing and studying will you discover and fully enjoy the richness of the game." Sets with bone tiles and bamboo backs were offered at between $10 and $30. A set of only bamboo cost from $4–$6 and for a complete wooden case in a tasteful box, an additional $2.50 had to be paid. Perry & Co. supplied a Dutch instruction book with the sets. Very soon, the mahjong sets flew out of the stores. Thousands were sold.

In Amsterdam the Netherlands Mah-Jongg League was founded, which gave demonstrations of the new game in crowded cafés. In living rooms and clubhouses, the sober Dutch surrendered themselves to the magic of the exotic mahjong. Tennis players joined the clubs during their winter hiatus and exchanged "topspin" and "volley" enthusiastically for "Chow" and "mahjong." The press was utterly amused with the new craze and came to take photographs. "Mahjong," the newspapers wrote, "has become like an infectious disease. Everyone wants to play it."

Also in their colonies, the Dutch played mahjong with devotion, so the *Indische Post* reported. According to the newspaper, the presence of Chinese servants gave rise to many amusing scenes: "A boy, who has to serve the players, forgot his work, looked with full attention to the game, let a glass full of cool drink fall down the neckline of her ladyship, when he couldn't resist to point out a stupid move to her. Gone is prestige. 'Oh, Missie you are much too stupid.' And the ladies played their game full of ardency with the servants in order to excel during the next mahjong drive and to be able to rely on Chinese sources during possible disputes about the playing rules."

The Netherlands was under the spell of mahjong when Joseph Babcock established an office of his Continental Mah-Jongg Sales Co. in Amsterdam. Babcock sold his sets in four varieties. All tiles were manually engraved and painted in China, his firm guaranteed. The most expensive set (the price is unknown) could hardly be distinguished from ivory. The set was stored in a splendid lacquer box with five drawers and white metal handles.

In the Netherlands mahjong is often played with deadly earnestness and much concentration.

J. P. Babcock's "Rules for Mah-jongg" (usually called "The Red Book") was included with each set. The booklet was also sold separately in bookstores. The playing rules of Babcock, however, differed from those of Perry. Thus, the Netherlands also was acquainted with differing playing rules. Although the differences were not dramatic, they were big enough to spread confusion in a country where churches splinter because of the least discrepancy. The debate ensued: How should mahjong really be played? What were the true rules?

Mah-Jongg.

Het groote succes is voor ons aanleiding **HEDENAVOND** nog een demonstratie te houden door 4 experts, in Café Neuf. Kalverstraat 41. Gasten zijn welkom! De aanwezigen der vorige week zullen wij thans gaarne als lid begroeten, om hen door **practische** lessen in Mah-Jongg verder in te wijden.

Neth. Mah-Jongg League.
2634

Mah-Jongg-demonstratie

met gelegenheid tot het stellen van vragen en debat, door 4 experts, op **Woensdagavond a. s.** in Café NEUF, Kalverstr. 41. Gasten welkom.
NETH. MAH-JONGG LEAGUE.
23

In these small advertisements the Netherlands Mah-Jongg League invites readers to their mahjong demonstrations by four experts.

The rule booklets of Babcock and Perry. The playing rules of Perry were a little bit more extensive than those of Babcock. Babcock and Perry used the same basic points for the several sequences but Perry also rewarded winning with the last tile for a draw and Robbing a Kong with 10 extra points, and doubled a completely Concealed Hand.

In November 1924 Babcock instituted legal proceedings against Perry & Co. and had the Perry handbook and its accompanying counting table confiscated on account of the copyright law. Babcock claimed that the mahjong playing rules were his intellectual property. He studied the game thoroughly in China. The game was so complicated that it could only be understood by the Chinese, but Babcock had transformed the game so that it became accessible for Western people. Moreover, he designed a counting system and had devised the name "Mah-Jongg," the lawyer declared. But the lawyer of Perry stated that F. L. Verster, one of the managing directors of the department stores, wrote the handbook "after extended study of the game and the treatises about it, received from China, America, and England." He handed the judge a series of booklets containing mahjong rules, of which none were written by Mr. Babcock.

The judge put Babcock in the wrong and declared that he would have never confiscated the Perry booklets if he had known the arguments of the American beforehand. The confiscation was lifted and Babcock was required to pay the costs of the trial. Perry advertised triumphantly: "At the moment we have again a variety of mahjong sets in the well-known boxes."

Faster than ever the mahjong sets and the booklets flew out of the Perry stores. The Dutch enjoyed themselves to the utmost with the exotic game. "The Game of the Thousand Wonders is in many circles a welcome pastime surpassing the game of bridge," the Perry firm cheered. "In contrast with the latter, everyone plays his own game with mahjong. Less skillful players do not spoil your hand!"

But the confusion about the playing rules in the Netherlands continued. Since the judge declared that Babcock's rules were not the only ones to be followed, and that there were other rules by which to play mahjong, a perfect Tower of Babel arose, creating such a clatter that not even the Netherlands Mah-Jongg League could be heard. Still more new rules arrived from mahjong-crazy America, causing even greater confusion. The weight of deciphering so many rules spoiled the joy of the game, and many mahjongers switched back to bridge. The mahjong

The first mahjong tournament in Holland was held in 1924 in Amsterdam and was sponsored by Perry & Co. There was a lot of interest in this tournament; sixty players participated.

sets went into the attics and the Netherlands Mah-Jongg League died a silent and inglorious death. In November 1925, a leading Dutch newspaper wrote cynically:

> Do you remember the mahjong craze of a year ago? Do you know that mahjong fabric came into the trade and also mahjong bonbons? That whoever was not orientated toward winds, characters, and flowers did not really count in a conversation? It lasted months and then all at once it was over. Completely over. No one is interested in mahjong anymore and whoever purchased a box full of ivory scrolls and flourishes for expensive money can put it aside with an unperturbed conscience. Nobody will give a penny for it. Mahjong is dead, long live rommé.

Playing Rules

What "rommé" was, nobody knows anymore, but mahjong is still played abundantly in Holland; at home, in mahjong clubs, and on mahjong drives. As a matter of fact, the Western mahjong revival started in the Netherlands and the first European championship was held there in 2005. Compared with basic mahjong the Dutch playing rules differ as follows:

- Bonus tiles are not used,
- Dead wall is not replenished,
- Winning is only possible with at least two Doubles,
- Large number of doubles for winner and losers,
- Funny winning pair (1-Bamboo with 1-Circles), and
- Eighteen special hands.

The Pung of Dragons and all Pungs provide two Doubles, sufficient for mahjong.

Participating at a tournament makes mahjong extra exciting. Mahjong tournaments take place throughout the year in Holland.

Settling Points

The points you score in the Netherlands are the same as in basic mahjong. However there is one odd addition:

Bird Eats Cake

If you complete a pair with 1-Circle instead of 1-Bamboo, it is rewarded with 10 extra points. This bizarre combination is called "Bird Eats Cake." You only get the 10 points if your 1-Bamboo (bird Pe-ling) is on your rack and you are waiting for mahjong. In this special case you may complete the pair with 1-Circle, the cake.

Example of Bird Eats Cake

Why the Bird Eats Cake

When one of the most famous generals from the Chinese history laid a 1-Circle beside a 1-Bamboo and announced mahjong with this unknown pair, the court was flabbergasted. Of course, a mighty man like this general had all rights not to lose and to play as treacherously as he liked, but to do it as openly and boldly did not show much refinement and good taste. The general, however, reproached the disconcerted audience and pointed out that the Great Creator gave many forms of life and of food, so that life is full of variations and full of surprises. It was out of respect for the Great Creator that the general made his extraordinary pair, and the bird Pe-ling had the right to profit from the bountiful gifts of life, so the general believed.

And therefore the general had given the big Circle, which is a big, round cake, to the little bird, so also this small creature should enjoy the richness of life and the gifts of nature. Nature and food belong inextricably to each other and that is why the bird and the cake form a perfect unity, the general declared. So his mahjong was completely in accordance with the regulations. Nobody, past or present, dared to contradict the general.

Doubles for All Players

The Dutch regulations are generous with doubles. Even the losers get quite a number of doubles. Doubling is almost the same as in basic mahjong:

Pung/Kong of Dragons	1 x
Pung/Kong of prevailing Winds	1 x
Pung/Kong of own Wind	1 x
One Suit with Honors	1 x
Terminals with Honors	1 x
Three concealed Pungs	1 x
Four concealed Pungs	2 x (A Kong counts always as a concealed Pung)
Only One Suit	3 x (Pure hand)
Four Kongs, exposed and concealed	3 x

For this hand you get two doubles. It consists namely of One Suit with Honors and of Terminals with Honors.

Doubles for the Winner

The winner may claim still more doubles for an exceptional hand and/or for the exceptional way he places his winning tile.

All Chows	1 x
All Pungs	1 x
All Simples	1 x
All concealed, also winning tile	2 x
Little Four Winds	1 x
Little Three Dragons	1 x
Robbing a Kong	1 x
Kong upon Kong	2 x
Winning with a loose tile	1 x *Kong with the Blossoming Flowers*
—if this tile is 5-Circles	3 x *Gathering the Plum Blossom from the Roof*
Winning with last tile from the wall	1 x *Winning from the Bottom of the Sea*
—if this tile is 1-Circles	3 x *Catching the Moon of the Bottom of the Sea*

1-Circle, when the last tile is self-drawn, gives this winning hand three extra doubles. That realizes a total of five doubles and six doubles if North is the prevailing Wind.

Special Hands

Finally there are nineteen special hands. The limit amounts are 2000 points. A Waiting Special Hand gives half the score. Here are some serpents you haven't seen until now.

Wriggling Snake

Pungs of 1s and 9s, Chows 3-4-5, 6-7-8, and pair 2-2 of one suit, or

Pung of 1s and 9s, Chows 2-3-4, 6-7-8, and pair 5-5 of one suit, or

Pung of 1s and 9s, Chows 2-3-4, 5-6-7, and pair 8-8 of one suit.
May be played exposed.
Score: half-limit.

Note: The Wriggling Snakes look very much like the Nine Gates, but its sequences can be formed while exposed at the table.

Wind Snake

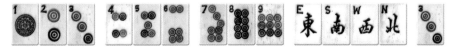

Tiles 1 through 9 of one suit, one of each Winds and a tile Double.
It should be played concealed, except for the winning tile.
Score: half limit.

Dragon Snake

Tiles 1 through 9 of one suit, one of each Dragons, and a pair of Winds.
It should be played concealed, except for the winning tile.
Score: half-limit.

Note: This serpent is rare and does not exist outside the Netherlands.

There are six kinds of twins. All have to be played concealed, except the winning tile.

Seven arbitrary twins form Seven pairs and score 250 points.

Seven pairs	Seven arbitrary pairs	one-eighth limit
Cleared pairs	Seven pairs of only one suit and Honors	one-fourth limit
Very cleared pairs	Only Terminals of one suit and Honors	half-limit
Pure pairs	Seven pairs of only one suit	half-limit
All Terminal pairs	Seven pairs of only Terminals	half-limit
Honors pairs	Seven pairs of only Honors	limit

Honors Pairs

With seven pairs of only Honor tiles you score the limit.

The other ten special hands are:

Nine Gates	limit
Four Concealed Kongs	limit
Thirteen Orphans	limit
Four Winds	limit
Three Dragons	limit
Jade Hand—pair can be of any green tiles	limit
Heads and Tails	limit
Peking Garden	half-limit
Heaven's Blessing	limit
Earth's Blessing	half-limit

House Rules

"We play it quite differently!"

"Then how?"

"With the faces down."

"Huh?"

"Otherwise you can see which tiles are discarded!"

"You have to see!"

"See? Remember, you mean!"

"Well, I have never heard of such a thing!"

"We always play like that. And it is very fun!"

There are hundreds of house rules and they all are passionately professed and defended. One plays with a dead wall of fourteen tiles, the other with sixteen tiles, or with no dead wall at all.

One plays always with bonus tiles, the other curses them. One places his concealed Kong completely concealed at the table, the other wants at least two tiles of such a Kong to be exposed. One plays with four Jokers, or with eight, and the other does not even know that Jokers exist.

"Jokers? What are they, for heaven's sake?"

Often mahjong is also played *blind*—the tiles are called by name and then discarded facedown. By doing this, you must rely on your memory because you cannot consult the discarded tiles again. It will become still harder if you want to change your tactic because you did of course not count all the tiles, but only the ones that were of importance for your purpose.

Each rule has its supporters and its opponents who accuse each other of not following the "correct" regulations.

Originally, however, mahjong was always played blind. Therefore mahjong tables had a hole in the middle where discarded tiles were dropped. Under the table, a small boy was seated who gathered those tiles and appeared only through the hole to build a new wall as soon as a game was over.

"Believe me!"

This book makes clear that there are no official regulations, that mahjong can be played in hundreds of ways and that only one rule always applies: agree beforehand about the regulations of play. House rules give a personal touch to mahjong. They make clear which features of mahjong are particularly appreciated.

Cheerful musicians and an acrobat adorn these bonus tiles of an ivory mahjong set from 1924.

Mahjongers about Mahjong

I learned mahjong from my dad, who in turn learned it from the Chinese aboard his ship. Due to its roots, naturally some coarseness had snuck into our version of mahjong. Thus we did not call Pung or Kong, but "Here that tile." And the other ones should discover for themselves if that was for a Pung or a Kong. 1-Bamboo was just "Pete" and 1-Circles was "big fat one"—yes, for those sailors.

—*Fred Koster, Holland*

When you become engaged to a Van Kuler you are obliged to learn the game of mahjong, otherwise the engagement won't last. So when I was acquainted with Rolf, my future husband, I was introduced to the game. When our children were engaged to be married, we asked the same of their fiancées. We still play each week with Rolf's parents (84 and 85 years old), who have maintained a remarkably clear mind from their mahjong habit.

—*Marja van Kuler, Holland*

FRANCE

In the winter of 1922–1923 the French came under the spell of the new Chinese game, which spread like a wildfire over Europe. Paris, after enjoying an exciting exposition about Tutankhamen, was eager for more exotica when mahjong came along. The Parisians fell in love with mahjong immediately, not because of the game itself but more because of its exotic charisma. The fashion world became instantly inspired by the new rage. "Heads are garnished with mahjong tiles, blouses are embroidered with mahjong patterns," the press reported from the French capital. "Umbrella handles, but also ladies' handbags, cigarettes holders, and so on show mahjong decorations. In France and also in Belgium it is now the height of fashion to possess a mahjong set. To play with it is not necessary. Only the more expensive sets are sold here."

An ornate drawer cabinet for a mahjong set of pure ivory tiles. The French appreciated such beautiful mahjong sets and cabinets as exquisitely decorated objects in their own right, as much as for their use in playing mahjong.

One of the fashion editors wrote with disdain about the source of inspiration of the French couturiers:

For a long time already we've had mahjong decorations on hats. Even that starts already to become a little bit "vieux jeu." Mahjong patterns on dresses and coats are something newer. Now the very latest mahjong novelty is announced, which this time is not a "nouveauté de Paris," but a "nouveauté de Londres"—mahjong stockings. Stockings with mahjong patterns with bold big placards, one or two beside or above each other, on each leg, unequal in size and even unequal in height as well. Sometimes there are even three pictures on one leg. Does it looks nice? Nice, what a question! Does that matter when something is fashionable?

Playing Rules

It will probably not be a surprise to learn that a people who focused on mahjong as an exotic objet d'art nowadays has rules that differ from what is common in other countries. Especially in the area of special hands, the French are richly and exclusively assorted. Almost everywhere in the game the French have small deviations.

Opening the Wall

The deviations begin with the opening of the wall. First East throws two dice to decide which Wind will open the wall. This throw also decides which Wind will be the prevailing Wind.

Example: East throws 3 and 1 for a total of 4. Then North has to open the wall and North will be the prevailing Wind during the first hand of the game.

Bonus Tiles

The walls are eighteen tiles long, because the bonus tiles also take part in the game.

Dead Wall

The dead wall is fourteen tiles. The tiles of the dead wall are stone dead. They do not take part in the game. Replacement tiles for a Kong or a bonus tile are drawn from the end of the live wall, to the right of the opening that marks the dead wall.

Concealed Kong

A French concealed Kong remains truly concealed. All tiles are put upside down on the table, so the other players remain uncertain about the identity of the tiles. A player does not reveal anything by claiming a Kong, and the tension remains. Certainly the player who is collecting a snake, and needs one of every tile of one suit, will have difficulties with such a fully concealed Kong.

Priority Rules

The priority rules for French mahjong also differ. In the case of a simultaneous announcement of a mahjong, a Pung mahjong has priority over a Chow mahjong and a Chow mahjong will go before a pair mahjong. When more players claim a Chow or a pair mahjong, then the player whose turn is first has the priority.

Because of their complicated rules, it is not easy to play the French version of mahjong. But if you find yourself at a French mahjong table, knowing these calls will help you. *Bonne chance,* good luck!

mah-jong	mahjong
familles: cercles, caractères, bambous	suits: Circles, Characters, Bamboos
vents: est, sud, ouest, nord	Winds: East, South, West, North
dragons: blanc, rouge, vert	Dragons: White, Red, Green
tuiles, honneurs supremes, honneurs	tiles, bonus tiles, Honor tiles
les fleurs, les saisons, un bouquet	the flowers, the seasons, a bouquet
les dés, les jetons, la réglette	the dice, the chips, the ruler
remise	draw
la main, la manche, l'ecart	the hand, the game, the discarded tile
paire, sequence, brelan, carré	pair, Chow, Pung, Kong
brelan naturel, brelan exposé	concealed Pung, exposed Pung
le mur, la colline	the wall, the dead wall
vent du joueur, vent dominant	own Wind, prevailing Wind
vent du tour	Wind of the round
un serpent, un grand jeu	a snake, a special hand
Je vous supplie: pas de grands jeux !	I beg of you: no special hands!

Settling Points

The French method of calculating points is also quite distinct. You will receive no points for an exposed pair of the prevailing Wind or for an exposed pair of Dragons.

You get the normal 20 points for a mahjong, but for self-drawn you get 5 points (instead of 2 points). For winning with an All Chow Hand you get 10 points.

If you win with 5-Circles you will get 100 extra points. The French call this "Picorer par le Coq d'Or," or "picking by the golden cock."

You can earn 500 extra points for Buried Treasure—a hand of only concealed Pungs/Kongs of one suit and/or Winds and Dragons.

Heaven's Blessing, mostly rewarded with the limit, gives you only 800 points in France and for Earth's Blessing, you will get 900 points.

An All Honors hand is rewarded with a meager 1,900 points.

Special Hands

The most peculiar aspect of the French style of play is the special hands. Some of them are similar to those used in the rest of the world, but mostly not. Curious combinations are in abundance, and where they came from or who invented them is a mystery. The special hands don't have a fixed value but range from 6000 points to 500 points (for Seven Pairs). Here they are:

Mahjong of the Emperor

Three concealed Kongs of Dragons and a pair of own Winds.
Except for the winning tile, it is played concealed.
Score: 6,000 points.
French name: Le mah-jong impérial.

Mahjong of the Mandarin

Three Pungs of Winds, a Chow of the same Winds, and a pair of Winds.
Except for the winning tile, it is played concealed.
Score: 5,000 points.
French name: Le mah-jong du mandarin.

Mahjong of the Crazy Monkey

Pung of Dragons, a "Chow" of Dragons, and a pair of own Winds.
Except for the winning tile, it is played concealed.
Score: 4,500 points.
French name: Le mah-jong du singe fou.

The Four Winds

Pungs/Kongs of the Four Winds and any pair.
It can be played exposed.
Score: 6,000 points.
French name: Le Quadruple bonheur domestique.

Imperial Jade

A hand of only green tiles, except for 3-Bamboo.
It can be played exposed.
Score: 3,600 points.
French name: La grande main verte majeure.

Big Jade

Pungs of Green Bamboos (except for 3-Bamboo) and a pair of Green Dragons.
It can be played exposed.
Score: 3,500 points.
French name: La grande main verte mineure.

Green and Red

Pungs of Red Bamboos and a "pair" formed by a Green Dragon and a Red
Dragon (the latter is an oddity since a pair is always formed by two of the same
tiles).
It can be played exposed.
Score: 3,400 points.
French name: La main verte et rouge.

The Foster Sons of the Great Dragon

Three Pungs/Kongs of 9s in each suit, a Pung of Dragons, and a pair of own
Winds.
It can be played exposed.
Score: 3,300 points.
French name: Les trois fils adoptifs du Dragon neuf.

The Foster Sons of the Little Dragon

Three Pungs/Kongs of 1s in each suit, a Pung of Dragons, and a pair of own
Winds.
It can be played exposed.
Score: 3,300 points.
French name: Les trois fils adoptifs du Dragon nain.

Jade String

Pung/Kong of 3-Bamboo, two Pungs/Kongs of Green Bamboos, and a pair of Green Bamboos.
It can be played exposed.
Score: 3,200 points.
French name: La petite main verte majeure.

Little Jade

Pung of 3-Bamboo, Pungs/Kongs of Green Bamboos, and a pair of Green Dragons.
It can be played exposed.
Score: 3,000 points.
French name: La petite main verte mineure.

Enemies

Two Pungs/Kongs of opposite Terminals of one suit, two Pungs/Kongs of opposite Winds, and a "pair" of the two other opposite Winds.
Except for the winning tile, it is played concealed.
Score: 3,000 points.
French name: Les ennemis.

Tempest

Two Pungs of Dragons and pairs of all four Winds.
Except for the winning tile, it is played concealed.
Score: 3,000 points.
French name: La tempête.

The Foster Sons of the Red Dragon
Pungs/Kongs of the same numbers in three different suits, a Pung of Red Dragons, and a pair of Winds.
It can be played exposed.
Score: 2,800 points.
French name: Les trois fils adoptifs du Dragon rouge.

The Great Siamese Sisters

Four Pungs with increasing numbers in one suit and a pair of Dragons.
It can be played exposed.
Score: 2,700 points.
French name: Les quatre grandes soeurs siamoises.

The Little Siamese Sisters
Four Pungs with increasing numbers in one suit and a pair of Winds.
It can be played exposed.
Score: 2,500 points.
French name: Les quatre petites soeurs siamoises.

Great Pairs
Pairs of all Honor tiles.
Except for the winning tile, it is played concealed.
Score: 2,500 points.
French name: Le triangle éternel.

The Foster Sons of the Wind
Pungs/Kongs of the same numbers in each suit, a Pung of Red Dragons, and a pair of Winds.
It can be played exposed.
Score: 2,400 points.
French name: Les trois fils adoptifs du vent.

The Three Dragons
Three Pungs/Kongs of Dragons, any Chow, and any pair.
It can be played exposed.
Score: 2,000 points.
French name: Les trois grands apôtres.

Winds and Dragons

Four Pungs/Kongs of only Honor tiles and any pair.
It can be played exposed.
Score: 1,900 points.
French name: Le mah-jong des vents et des Dragons.

Nine Gates
Two Pungs of Terminals, a sequence of 2 through 8, and one Double tile, all in one suit.
Except for the winning tile, it is played concealed.
Score: 1,800 points.
French name: Le main pleine de neuf pièces.

Royal Pung
Three Pungs with equal numbers in each suit, Pung Dragons, and a pair of own Winds.
Except for the winning tile, it ought to be played concealed.
Score: 1,800 points.
French name: Le Pung royal.

Rose of Winds

Two sequences of the Four Winds and two sequences of the Three Dragons. Except for the winning tile, it is played concealed.
Score: 1,700 points.
French name: La rose des vents.

Pure Pairs

Seven pairs of Honor tiles.
Except for the winning tile, it is played concealed.
Score: 1,700 points.
French name: Les sept muses du poète chinois.

Thirteen Orphans

One of all Honor and Terminal tiles and one tile Double.
Except for the winning tile, it is played concealed.
Score: 1,600 points.
French name: Les treize lanternes merveilleuses.

Big Snake

Sequence 1 through 9 of one suit, Pung of Dragons or Winds, and a pair of Dragons.
Except for the winning tile, it is played concealed.
Score: 1,500 points.
French name: Le grand serpent.

Jewel Snake

Sequence 1 through 9 of one suit, Pung of the related Dragons, and a pair of Honor tiles.

Except for the winning tile, it is played concealed.
Score: 1,400 points.
French name: La main de diamant (for Circles), La main d'émeraude (for Bamboos), and La main de rubis (for Characters).

Dragon Snake
Sequence 1 through 9 of always changing suits, one tile of each Dragon, and a pair of own Winds.
Except for the winning tile, it is played concealed.
Score: 1,400 points.
French name: Le serpentin des Dragons.

Swerving Wind
Three related Pungs (equal numbers and different suits), one of each Wind, and one Wind Double.
Except for the winning tile, it is played concealed.
Score: 1,400 points.
French name: Le triangle venteux.

Noble Hand

Three Pungs of one suit, a Pung of the related Dragons, and a pair of the same suit.
Except for the winning tile, it is played concealed.
Score: 2,500 points.
French name: La main précieuse.

Noble Pairs
Six pairs of one suit and a pair of the related Dragons.
Except for the winning tile, it is played concealed.
Score: 1,300 points.
French name: Les paires de shozum.

Little Wind Snake

Sequence 1 through 9 of always changing suits, one tile of each Wind, and one Red Dragon.
Except for the winning tile, it is played concealed.
Score: 1,200 points.
French name: Le serpentin des quatre vents.

Variant: Instead of the Red Dragon every Honor tile is allowed. The hand earns then 1000 points.

Big Brothers

Sequence 1 through 9 of one suit, a Pung of Winds/Dragons, and a pair of own Winds.
Except for the winning tile, it is played concealed.
Score: 1,200 points.
French name: Les grands frères.

Peking Garden

Sequence 1 through 7 of one suit, one tile of each Wind, and one tile of each Dragon.
Except for the winning tile, it is played concealed.
Score: 1,100 points.
French name: Le jardin de Gretos.

Little Snake

Sequence 1 through 9 of one suit, one tile of each Wind, and an Honor tile.
Except for the winning tile, it is played concealed.
Score: 1,000 points.
French name: Le petit serpent.

Wind Pairs

A pair of each Wind and a pair of each suit.

Except for the winning tile, it is played concealed.

Score: 1,000 points.

French name: Les paires venteuses.

Wind Pungs

A Pung/Kong of each suit, one of each Wind, and one Wind Double.

Except for the winning tile, it is played concealed.

Score: 800 points.

French name: Les brelans venteux.

Chinese Hand

A Pung of 1s, a sequence 2 through 8, a Pung of 9s, and one tile Double.

Except for the winning tile, it is played concealed.

Score: 700 points.

French name: La main chinoise.

Poor Soul

Sequence 1 through 7, one tile of each Wind, and a Pung of Dragons.

Except for the winning tile, it is played concealed.

Score: 700 points.

French name: Le joueur maladroit.

Six Orphans

1s and 9s of each suit, a sequence of 2 through 8 of one suit, and one tile Double.

Except for the winning tile, it is played concealed.

Score: 700 points.

French name: La main pleine de neuf pièces.

Royal Chow

Three Royal Chows of different suits, one of each Dragon, and a pair of own Winds.
Except for the winning tile, it is played concealed.
Score: 600 points.
French name: Le Chow royal.

Little Dragon Snake

Sequence 1 through 7 and a Double of one tile, a Pung of Dragons, and a Pung of own Winds.
Except for the winning tile, it ought to be played concealed.
Score: 500 points.
French name: Les sept lanternes du palais.

Wind Chows

A Chow of every suit, one of each Wind, and one Wind Double.
Except for the winning tile, it is played concealed.
Score: 500 points.
French name: Les Chow venteux.

Seven Pairs

Seven pairs.
Except for the winning tile, it is played concealed.
Score: 500 points.
French name: Le main des paires.

GERMANY

The mahjong craze of the 1920s did not take hold in Germany. After the First World War the country was poor and the import of luxury goods was forbidden. To play the game Germans had to make mahjong sets themselves. But their sets lacked the exotic allure of the Eastern sets. They came with ugly wooden tiles and, moreover, were quite expensive. Despite Germany's weakened postwar economy, German workers were still much more expensive than Chinese workers. The rest of Europe was not interested in the pricey unattractive German product. German manufacturers could not compete with the beautiful Chinese sets and their enthusiasm faded quickly. The market was too small and the consumer too poor. The "Game of the Thousand Possibilities" got little chance there.

Happily, mahjong is popular in present day Germany. The restrictive importation regulations were lifted after the Second World War and delicate mahjong sets are now as easy to buy in Germany as elsewhere in Europe.

The Internet has promoted interest in the game, though many still prefer to play the noncyber way. "When we are seated around the table, the tea or wine glimmers

A post–WWI mahjong set of German making. Wooden tiles were placed in simple cardboard boxes.

in the glasses and the most beautiful tiles are stacked in a wall, an ambiance pervades the air, one that cannot be reproduced by a computer screen," a German mahjonger reports on an Internet site devoted to the game. "Mahjong fascinates every type of player, the strategist as well as the tactician, the thinker as well as the adventurer."

The mahjong craze of the 1920s was a boon for the small Chinese merchants. Those who once sold peanuts in the street for a living were happy to be consulted as experts in the field of mahjong, and to exchange their peanut boxes for Chinese gowns.

Playing Rules

Germany did not participate in the competition over the playing rules, which followed on the introduction of mahjong in the West. So, for the most part, Germans use standard rules. Still there are some abnormalities.

Limit

There is not only a limit of 5000 points as a maximum score but there is also a minimum of 100 points. The high limit is to promote the forming of special hands. The minimum of 100 points prevents you from reaching mahjong too easily. So you may not get a mahjong if your hand has less than 100 points.

When playing with Germans, you have to count throughout the game to see if you have reached the 100-point minimum needed to declare mahjong. (Normally you need only count the number of necessary Doubles.)

Bonus Tiles

The bonus tiles are used in the game. The sides of the wall are thus eighteen tiles long.

Dead Wall

The dead wall counts eight tiles and is marked by two loose tiles, which are laid on the first and third pair. East is responsible for replenishing the dead wall so that it always consists of eight tiles. Only he is allowed to draw a loose tile when a player needs an extra tile after a Kong or a bonus tile.

Dangerous Discards

A player can also be forced to pay for the others. This happens with dangerous play. If you have exposed three combinations of a high-scoring mahjong (or, for the Chinese who play for money, a *lucrative* mahjong), the other players are not allowed to discard the winning tile. When it does happen, and the discarded tile does indeed cause the high-scoring mahjong, then the guilty player has to pay on behalf of the other players.

Dangerous play arises when a player has:
- Three combinations of one suit;
- Three combinations of Honor tiles;
- Two combinations of one suit and one combination of Honor tiles; and
- Three combinations of a Special Hand.

Example:

North has a Kong of West Winds and two Pungs of Bamboos exposed on the table. It is now dangerous play to discard a Bamboo tile.

Despite that South discards 8-Bamboo, after which North goes mahjong.

Exposed:

Concealed:

With this hand North earns a score of 208 points. South has to pay for all players: 416 for East, 208 for himself, and 208 for West, in total 816 points. East and West settle their scores between them.

A player isn't always punished for dangerous play. Here are the instances when you may discard a dangerous tile with impunity:
- You have a Waiting Hand;
- You discard the same tile as the player before you; and
- You have only dangerous tiles.

Note: The dangerous play rule was invented to protect players from a reckless or distracted player who discards tiles without thinking, thus causing the other players to suffer from his careless behavior. In practice, however, it turns out that the dangerous play rule often has an opposite effect. It decreases the chances of the other players to obtain a decent mahjong because they are restricted in discarding dangerous tiles, while the reckless player can discard what he wants. The situation becomes even worse when there are two dangerous plays in force; then the other players have hardly any choice about their discards.

It is clear from the example that dangerous play applies even for a mahjong that earns only 208 points. The Germans may only go out when they have a minimum of 100 points.

German for Mahjongers

It can happen that a German invites you for a game of mahjong. With the vocabulary below you don't have to be dumbfounded.

| Mah Jongg | mahjong |
| Farbe: Kreise, Schrift, Bambus | Suits: Circles, Characters, Bamboos |

Winde: Ostwind, Südwind, Westwind, Nordwind	Winds: East, South, West, North
weisse, rote, grüne Drache	White, Red, Green Dragon
Steine, Hasardsteine, Trumpfsteine	tiles, bonus tiles, Honor tiles
Blume, Jahreszeiten, Strauss	flowers, seasons, bouquet
Würfel, Zählstäbchen, Bank	dice, chips, ruler
Remis	draw
Hand, Spiel, abgeworfen Stein	hand, game, discarded tile
Paar, Chow, Pung, Kong	pair, Chow, Pung, Kong
verdeckte Pung, offene Pung	concealed Pung, exposed Pung
Mauer, tote Mauer, Ersatzstein	wall, dead wall, loose tile
eigener Wind, vorherrschende Wind	own Wind, prevailing Wind
Windrunde	Wind of the round
Schlange, Spezialhand	snake, special hand
Störspiel	dangerous play
Entschuldigung, Frau Müller, aber Sie haben eine tote Hand.	I'm afraid, Miss Johnson, you have a dead hand.

Special Hands

You will find some new varieties among the German special hands.

Flush

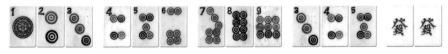

Chows 1-2-3, 4-5-6, 7-8-9, and an arbitrary Chow, all in one suit, plus a pair of Winds/Dragons or a pair of the same suit.
It can be played exposed.
Score: half-limit.
German name: Flush.

Royal Flush

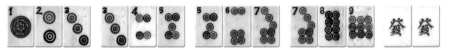

Chows 1-2-3, 3-4-5, 5-6-7, 7-8-9, all of one suit, plus a pair of Winds/Dragons or a pair of the same suit.
It can be played exposed.
Score: limit.
German name: Royal Flush.

Heaven's Ladder (1)

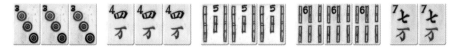

Four succeeding Pungs and a succeeding pair of arbitrary suits, plus a pair of Winds/Dragons or a pair of the same suit.
It can be played exposed.
Score: limit.
German name: Himmelsleiter.

Heaven's Ladder (2)

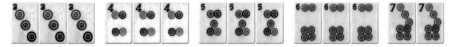

Four succeeding Pungs and a succeeding pair, all of one suit, plus a pair of Winds/Dragons or a pair of the same suit.
It can be played exposed.
Score: double limit.
German name: Himmelsleiter.

Climbing Snake

Four odd Pungs and a pair of Terminals, all of one suit, plus a pair of Winds/Dragons or a pair of the same suit.

It can be played exposed.

Score: limit.

German name: Sich windende Schlange.

Germans also play with the following special hands:

Nine Gates	limit
Jade Hand	double limit
Four Kongs	limit
Pure pairs	double limit
Thirteen Orphans	double limit
Four Winds	double limit
Three Dragons	half-limit
All Terminals	limit
Heaven's Blessing	limit
Earth's Blessing	limit

ITALY

In Italy mahjong is played with enthusiasm and mahjong tournaments are organized frequently, most of the time by the Federazione Italiana Mah-Jong.

Playing Rules

Notable rules are:

- A Kong can be claimed even after a player goes out. He is not allowed to draw an extra tile from the dead wall.
- If the first discard of all four players is the same Wind, that hand is immediately called a draw.
- A Waiting Hand can be announced to get an extra double.
- If you draw the last tile from the wall and it is not your winning tile, then you don't have to discard a tile and it is a draw.

Seating Arrangements

Using two dice, the players determine their places at the table. The player with the highest throw becomes East, the next one South, and so on. East casts two dice to decide where the wall will be opened. The first throw decides the Wind of the round. If she, for instance, throws 11, then West becomes the prevailing Wind. When East loses her turn because she does not go out, then the prevailing Wind also changes—it becomes North.

The wall designated by East's first throw is opened. If East, for instance, cast 10, then South has to make the second throw. If South now, for instance, throws 11, then the counting continues past eighteen tiles at the side of South.

Bonus Tiles

Since bonus tiles are used in the play, the walls are eighteen tiles long. Every bonus tile gives you 4 points. Your own bonus tile gives a double. A series of four bonus tiles gives also one double. Replacement tiles are drawn from the dead wall. The dead wall is not replenished.

Announcing a Waiting Hand

When you have a Waiting Hand with only one possibility of going out, then you can announce it. This is called *Riichi* or *Richi*. If you succeed in going out, then you get an extra double, though there are some conditions. There have to be more than eight tiles in the live wall. You may not change anything in your hand and all the tiles you draw, except for the winning tile, have to be discarded immediately. This includes bonus tiles and any other tiles that would improve your hand.

Counting

To make counting of the scored points easier, the Italians always mark their concealed Pungs and Kongs with a crossed tile. Your own bonus tile is also marked that way.

A concealed Pung, a concealed Kong, and your own bonus tiles

Doubles for All

Besides the usual doubles, you also get a double for:
- Three equal Chows, in one or three suits;
- Four equal Chows, in one or three suits;
- Snake, in one or three suits; and
- Chained Snake, in one or three suits.

A Chained Snake—the combinations overlap each other

Doubles for the Winner

Besides the usual doubles, the winner is entitled to an extra double:
- If you go out before fifteen tiles are played, including the discarded tiles (bonus tiles are not included);
- If you win with a tile of which only one was still in play;

- If you draw the winning tile from the wall;
- If you draw the last tile;
- If you have announced Riichi; and
- If all of your four combinations are exposed on the table and you win with a pair. (The Italians call this *imbottigliato*, meaning bottled.)

The winner gets two doubles:
- If he has only Pungs/Kongs.

Special Hands

There are eleven special hands but different limits:

Nine Gates	3000 points
Heaven's Blessing	3000 points
All Kongs	3000 points
Four Winds	2000 points

No difference is made between the Little Four Winds (three Pungs of Winds and a Pair of Winds) and the Four Winds (four Pungs of Winds).

Three Dragons	2000 points
Thirteen Orphans	2000 points
Little Snake	1000 points

Snake of one suit, one of each Wind, and an arbitrary last tile; when possible it can be played exposed.

All Suits Snake	2000 points

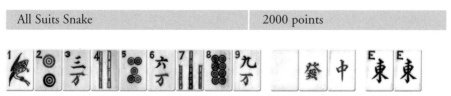

Snake of three suits, always in the same order, three Dragons, and a pair of prevailing or own Winds. The winning tile may be drawn from the table.

Siamese Snake	1,000 points

Two Knitted Snakes 1 through 7. The winning tile may be drawn from the table.

All Honor pairs	1,000 points
Pure pairs	1,000 points

Italian for Mahjongers

It is said of Italians that they have hot-blooded natures that could easily ignite in the heat of a mahjong game. Therefore it is wise in such a situation to have the right words at hand, although Italians hardly talk during playing.

mah-jongg	mahjong
colori: circoli, caratteri, bambù	suits: Circles, Characters, Bamboos
venti: Est, Sud, Ovest, Nord	Winds: East, South, West, North
drago bianco, rosso, verde	White, Red, Green Dragon
pedine, fiori, pedine di testa	tiles, bonus tiles, Major tiles
fiori, stagioni, bouquet of rosa	flowers, seasons, bouquet
dado, fiche, steccha	dice, chips, ruler
a monte	draw
mano, gioco, pedina scartata	hand, game, discarded tile
coppia, scala, tris, poker	pair, Chow, Pung, Kong
tris coperto, tris scoperto	concealed Pung, exposed Pung
muro, tetto, pedina dal tetto	wall, dead wall, loose tile
vento di giro/di round	Wind of the round
serpente, grande giocho	snake, special hand
Scusi Signore, Lei è Grandissimo Signore	Excuse me Sir, but your hand has too many tiles

NEVER SAY NEVER

Mahjong is a game for four players, but you might find yourself on occasion with two, three, or even five players. Though mahjong is designed for four players, the game can still be played with the following adjustments. Never say never!

An illustration on an old American mahjong box showing Chinese gentlemen caught up in the Game of Ten Thousand Possibilities

Five Players

It is played with the standard number of tiles—136 or 144—depending on whether you want to play with or without the bonus tiles.

Seating Arrangements

The five players throw the dice in turn. The player who threw the least eyes will be the dreamer and does not take part in the first hand.

If you used concealed Wind tiles to allocate the seats at the table then you have to add a Red Dragon tile. He who picks the Red Dragon is the dreamer.

The other four players play their first hand. When this hand is over the dreamer becomes East and North becomes the new dreamer. The other players move up one Wind: South becomes West and West becomes North.

Variant: To keep the dreamer from waiting too long, you can agree that North should leave after every hand to become the dreamer, also when East wins or a draw occurs.

Settling Points

The four players settle their scored points. The dreamer does not participate.

Variant: The dreamer does participate in the settling. He does not have to pay, but he receives from each of the three losing players 2 points that are doubled the same number of times that the winner's score was doubled. East has to pay one more double if he belongs to the losers. There is a limit of six doubles.

Example: North wins with three doubles.

East pays the dreamer four doubles of 2 points = 32 points.
South and West pay the dreamer each three doubles of 2 points = 16 points.
North, who won, pays nothing.
So the dreamer gets 64 points.

Variant: Under the American Maj rules the dreamer becomes a bettor. He bets who will win the next hand. If he is right then he receives from the three losers as many points as the winner. If he is wrong, then the dreamer pays the winner as many points as the losers have to pay.

Five Hands

A Wind is played if any player has been East one time. This means that for each Wind, five hands are played, but since one player sits out on each hand, each player plays four hands per Wind. In total four Winds are played, one for every Wind.

Variant: For the sake of balance a fifth round can be played, the round of the Red Dragon. When a Red Dragon round is played, Red Dragon replaces what is normally a prevailing Wind. A pair of Red Dragons then earns 4 points and a Pung/Kong of Red Dragons gives an extra double, or two doubles in total.

The usual playing rules are obeyed.

Three Players

If there are only three players and they want still to play mahjong, the game will lose its sophisticated balance. Chances and scores become higher and the tension lessens. But yes, it is still better to play mahjong with three than not to play mahjong at all.

Number of Tiles

North does not participate in this game. The four North Wind tiles and all the Bamboo tiles are removed. The number of tiles will be ninety-six or one hundred, depending on whether you play without or with bonus tiles. A Wind consists of three hands and a complete game of four Winds.

Variant: If you play with bonus tiles there will be a better balance if you also remove North's two bonus tiles. These are the tiles marked with the number 4: Winter and Bamboo.

Building the Wall

The wall is built in a triangle or in a square as desired. If you choose the triangle the walls are sixteen tiles long. If you play with all bonus tiles East has to build a wall of sixteen tiles, but South and West make walls of seventeen tiles.

Fewer Special Hands

For the rest the game, the usual rules apply. Because one Wind and one suit are missing, some special hands are impossible—such as Four Winds, Windy Snake, Winds Snake, Peking Garden, and Thirteen Orphans.

Also the Charleston becomes difficult but not impossible: the player who has to exchange with the missing Wind exchanges with the wall at that side. Therefore the wall has to be built in a square.

Limitations

When playing with three the chances of forming combinations are higher. Therefore limitations such as the following can be applied:
- No exposed Chows;
- No Chows at all;
- A dead wall of twenty tiles.

Expansions

In America, the land of the unlimited possibilities, the Wind tiles that have been removed from the set are sometimes added as an extra series of Dragons. Then a Pung or Kong of North Winds raises an extra double and a pair of North Winds produces 2 points.

Two Players

All tiles remain in the play. The players are East and West and also take care of the obligations of South and North. They build a square that is opened and broken down in the usual way.

Beforehand it is agreed when a mahjong is permitted:
- With at least four Doubles; or
- With a special hand; or
- With a half-limit.

The game follows the usual rules, but Chows are forbidden.

The scoring system is the same. Both the winner and the loser pay; they settle their scores. Because East replaces South, he pays double and receives double if South is the prevailing Wind. The same applies to West, which replaces North.

Mahjong for two players is useful when first learning the game. With this variant beginners can get used to the tiles and the terminology without feeling embarrassed when making mistakes or uncertain moves in the company of more experienced players. At the same time, this version of play can be filled with tension and excitement for experienced players since they can concentrate on beautiful combinations with very high scores.

Variant: The North and South Winds are removed, and also the related bonus tiles, so you are playing with 124 tiles. East/South builds walls of 16 tiles and West/North builds walls of 15 tiles.

One Player

Having a burning desire to play mahjong but no one to play with is the saddest thing in the whole world. But thanks to the computer you *can* play mahjong. Many good software programs are available and you can use the Internet to play with people all over the world. Keep this book at hand because playing rules do differ.

Killing Time

The mahjong tiles lay on the table but you may be waiting for another player or for something else. You can pass time with Turtle Chase, a game that takes no longer than a few minutes. It can be played with one, two, or three players.

Every player chooses a suit and thoroughly shuffles his thirty-six tiles facedown. Then everyone forms a rectangle of four closed rows of nine tiles. You then randomly pick a tile from the upper row. If it is for instance 7-Bamboo, then you put this tile faceup above the fourth column. Push the row carefully downward, so that one tile is pushed out from the pattern.

The other players simultaneously do the same, pushing downward the column that is indicated by the drawn tile.

The tile that is pushed out of the bottom is exposed. Suppose it is 7-Bamboo, then you place this tile above the seventh column and you push this column downward, so that another tile appears at the bottom. You continue in this way until all tiles are exposed or until you cannot progress anymore and some tiles stay concealed. The number of concealed tiles determines the score. If for instance five tiles remain unexposed you pay the other players a 5 point penalty. The other players do the same.

If you succeed in exposing all tiles, then the other players pay you double their losses.

Turtle Chase can be played as long as you like, until you are bored, or until the fourth player has finally brought the drinks and snacks to the table.

Cards

There is also a variant of mahjong that you play using cards. The cards have the same pictures as the tiles. The only difference is that you cannot build a wall with them. Often players have difficulty holding thirteen or fourteen cards in their hands; however, there are boards on which you can sort your cards without revealing them.

The play follows the usual pattern. The cards are shuffled and put in a pile on the table. The last fourteen cards are placed crosswise; they aren't used in the game. The players pick up their thirteen cards in the usual way: three times four cards and finally one card, whereafter the leading player draws his fourteenth card.

Whoever draws a bonus tile or announces a Kong picks an extra card from the pile. The cards are openly discarded on a second pile. Of the discarded cards only the last card is visible. When the fourteenth transverse card is reached, it is a draw.

Mahjong cards can replace mahjong tiles, but give yourself some time to get used to playing with them.

QUICK MAHJONG REFERENCE

Quick Reference—Mahjong Terms

Mahjong

Four sets (Chows, Pungs, or Kongs) and a pair

Chow

Sequence of three successive tiles

Pung

Triplet of three matching tiles

Kong

Quad of four matching tiles

Pair

Two matching tiles

Quick Reference—Tiles

Three suits

Circles, Bamboos, Characters

Four Winds

East, South, West, North

Three Dragons

White, Green, Red,

Eight Bonus Tiles

Flowers, seasons

Quick Reference—Types of Tiles

Honor tiles

Winds and Dragons

Terminals

1s and 9s

Simple tiles

2 through 8

HANDY DOUBLING TABLE FOR BASIC MAHJONG

Use this table to quickly calculate scores when playing basic mahjong (see pp. 29–50).

	1 x	2 x	3 x	4 x	5 x	6 x	7 x
20	40	80	160	320	640	1280	2560
22	44	88	176	352	704	1408	2816
24	48	96	192	384	768	1536	3072
26	52	104	208	416	832	1664	3328
28	56	112	224	448	896	1792	3584
30	60	120	240	480	960	1920	3840
32	64	128	256	512	1024	2048	4096
34	68	136	272	544	1088	2176	4352
36	72	144	288	576	1152	2304	4608
38	76	152	304	608	1216	2432	4864
40	80	160	320	640	1280	2560	5120
42	84	168	336	672	1344	2688	5376
44	88	176	352	704	1408	2816	5632
46	92	184	368	736	1472	2944	5888
48	96	192	384	768	1536	3072	6144
50	100	200	400	800	1600	3200	6400
52	104	208	416	832	1664	3328	6656
54	108	216	432	864	1728	3456	6912
56	112	224	448	896	1792	3584	7168
58	116	232	464	928	1856	3712	7424
60	120	240	480	960	1920	3840	7680

ACKNOWLEDGMENTS

For the realization of *The Great Mahjong Book* I am grateful to many friends, acquaintances, and total strangers, who became friends. Without their help and guidance, this book would not have become a great book of mahjong:

Ed Walters, Publishing Director of Tuttle Publishing, who saw the possibilities of widening the audience for this book, which was originally published in a Dutch edition;

Holly Jennings, the editor who saw the book through to bound book, and who worked steadfastly to Americanize my English, a worthy task since Dutch is my first language;

Kathy Wee and **Daniel Urban** for their beautiful design of the interior and cover of this edition; **Kirsten Bjorneboe** for her design of the interior of the original Dutch edition, which was the basis for this book's layout;

Martin Rep, editor of the independent internet newspaper Mahjong NEWS, who read, commented on, and corrected all versions of the Dutch edition, and remained constantly enthusiastic;

Sjek Strik, who proved himself to be the Dutch Riichi specialist;

Ryan Morris, a mahjong consultant, expert especially in Japanese Riichi and Chinese Official play, who, in the course of reading the English manuscript, raised good questions, provided excellent comments, and helped in places to smooth out my ofttimes awkward English syntax;

John Eberhardt, who provided me with unique illustrations;

Jim May, who generously donated much material from his internet Mah Jong Museum;

Ria Rep, my lifetime inspiration and supporter.

Jelte Rep
December 2006

INDEX